The Comprehensive Handbook of Constructivist Teaching

From Theory to Practice

The Comprehensive Handbook of Constructivist Teaching

From Theory to Practice

James Pelech, Ed.D.
Author

Gail Pieper, Ph.D.
Editor

Brenda: Your ideas and "soul" are in this Book. I am thrilled to call you "friend" and "colleague"

Jim Pelech
Oct 22, 2010

≡IAP

INFORMATION AGE PUBLISHING, INC.
Charlotte, NC • www.infoagepub.com

Library of Congress Cataloging-in-Publication Data

Pelech, James.
  The comprehensive handbook of constructivist teaching : from theory to
practice / James Pelech, Gail Pieper.
     p. cm.
  Includes bibliographical references.
  ISBN 978-1-60752-374-1 (pbk.) – ISBN 978-1-60752-375-8 (hardcover) –
ISBN 978-1-60752-376-5 (e-book)
  1. Constructivism (Education) 2. Teaching. 3. Teachers–Training of. I.
Pieper, Gail W. II. Title.
  LB1590.3P45 2010
  371.102–dc22

                                                              2009047561

Printed in the United States of America

Contents

Acknowledgements

First and foremost, I want to thank my wife, Gwen, for all her support. She really is the best at multi-tasking. She has been a wife, advocate, confidant, cheerleader, and best friend, and she does all of these things at the same time.

My son, Chris, has been a great inspiration. He has really shown me the "never quit" spirit. Hey Chris, the best is yet to come.

Rich Shewmake, my best friend, must be recognized for setting the standard on friendship. Well buddy, we just got through another "adventure."

To Dr. Alan Gorr, my Dean, thanks for believing in me.

To Dr. MeShelda Jackson, my Department Chair, I want to thank you for all of your encouragement.

To all my teaching colleagues in the School Education at Benedictine University, I have to let you know that all of you are in this book. Your influence on me has been tremendous, and your thoughts and ideas are the ingredients that I mixed together to create this book.

I want to give Sally Shore of Benedictine University special thanks for her work on the pictures and diagrams and for all her support over the years.

I want to thank Joyce Cecchi of Benedictine University for her friendship, support, and her ability to make all negative things seem positive.

To all the students I have had the privilege of interacting with over the years; I just want to say thanks for showing me what it really means to learn. All of you are the reasons teaching has been a "great gig."

—Jim Pelech

1

Getting a Head Start on Our Constructivist Practice

What do the following, the first a geometry problem, the second a definition question, and the third a manual writing exercise, have in common?

A group of high-school geometry students walk into a classroom and look at the screen in the front of the room. At each desk is a copy of a letter from a lawyer stating that in the recent lawsuit they filed, the defendant has come up with two possible settlements. One is to acquire the irregularly shaped parcel of land (shown on the overhead), which can then be sold for $1,500 an acre. The second settlement is to just take $350,000. After going over the letter and the diagram on the overhead of the parcel of land, the teacher gets students into pairs and has the students discuss what they must know in order to solve this situation. One student discusses his answer for thirty seconds. Then they switch roles. The teacher then asks students to come to the board and write down what they learned from their partner.

A college course in measurement and evaluation is studying the concept of validity. As students walk into the classroom, they notice that at each desk is a stack of five index cards. The teacher explains that he will say a word or phrase and then the students will write down five things that come to mind, putting one response on each

The Comprehensive Handbook of Constructivist Teaching, pages 1–5

card. Then the teacher says "validity." The students then get in groups of two or three, and decide on the three words or phrases that they all believe are most indicative of the group's feelings. A spokesperson from each group is chosen and puts these on the board. The teacher leads a discussion on how to put these words or phrases into categories.

Students are told that they will review the topic they just studied and that there will be a test on it in two days. The teacher gets students into pairs to create a manual titled "(Topic that they are studying)...for Dummies." The teacher tells the class that they are to use their imagination on this and to create what they would consider as the ideal study aid. The students are told that they can use this for the test. The teacher continuously goes throughout the room, and when he observes that all groups are on their way to developing the manual, he announces, "Have one partner go to the next group and learn what that group is doing." The "rover" goes back to his group and discusses what he has learned and how his group could use these ideas in their manual. The teacher then tells the other partner to rotate two places and replicate the same action as before. At the end of the "Dummies Manual activity" students are asked to write about the following prompts: What did you learn about...from this project? What did you learn about related areas, such as problem solving, working with another?

The three scenarios each involve Constructivist activities. In this book, you will learn about the Constructivist philosophy. But even if you are not interested in the theory of Constructivism, you will find the Constructivist teaching strategies presented here useful—whether you are involved in teaching on the elementary, high school, or college level and whether you are teaching basic arithmetic, science, or English.

Let us look again at the three scenarios. From them we can identify the following characteristics. First, they show us *how students learn.* Constructivism emphasizes interaction. Students learn from each other. And they learn best in groups, especially small groups.

A second feature these scenarios show is *what materials work best* for students. Constructivism is not an abstract philosophy; it emphasizes working in the real world. Students participate in topics from the real world. They work on what they already know. And they learn through both visuals and discussion.

Third, the scenarios show *outcomes.* Constructivism is a learning tool, and as such a tool it emphasizes results. Students make predictions and create their own solutions and hypotheses. Moreover, the students monitor their learning.

These activities represent only a small sampling of constructivist teaching strategies. While the purpose of this book is to present constructivist principles and guidelines and then provide teaching strategies based on these, we recognize that you may want results now, or at least tomorrow! We promise to meet this need.

In the remainder of this book, we will offer many more exercises, some of which will help sharpen your understanding of Constructivist principles, some of which will illustrate the wide range of applicability of Constructivist concepts, and some of which will satisfy your need for activities to use in your classroom—or in your life.

This book is intended to enable you, by using discrete steps, to translate the Constructivist philosophy into a practical tool for the classroom. While we have "gotten your appetite wet," the rest of the book presents the process for developing your own Constructivist philosophy. In the remainder of this book we present background on the philosophy and its principles, followed by chapters that translate those principles into concrete, observable student and teacher behaviors. This includes teaching strategies, assessment strategies, and professional development strategies.

But let us conclude this chapter with an exercise you can start with immediately. I've used this exercise successfully to conduct a review session in a geometry class and in a trigonometry class.

CONSTRUCTIVIST ACTIVITY 1.1:
Making School "More Authentic"—Skills

Description: While teachers, administrators, and school boards are besieged with the requirement to have students pass tests, many employers, parents, and college professors bemoan the reading and writing skills of students. On the other side of the coin, contemporary students often lose interest quickly in school subjects.

One solution is to connect the content of a school course with another medium with which the students are comfortable: the newspaper, perhaps. This exercise asks students to write a newspaper article that summarizes the topic they have just completed studying: the hypotenuse leg theorem for right triangles. The students are likely to react with disbelief: How could anyone write a newspaper article about such a boring, and obtuse, subject? Students were required to imagine that they are newspaper reporters covering this "case," and write a newspaper story on "proving right triangles congruent." Here students are using writing skills to create a review of "right triangle congruency."

Outcome: Following is an example of actual student work and is an excellent example of the Constructivist philosophy. Two students created this product together; they used real-world materials such as markers and crayons. In this case this is their version of the summary of the topic. Lastly,

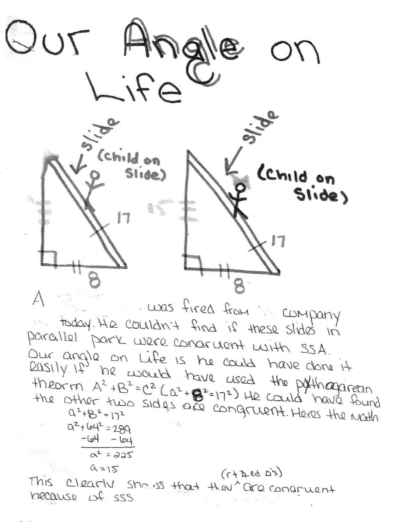

Figure 1.1

the outcome is a personal product that is authentic in nature, in that it is a product used in everyday life (a newspaper article). Figure 1.1 shows student work.

   Note: This example presents authenticity in terms of the skill needed to create the final outcome. Authenticity can also come in the form of the context of the assignment. The following activities illustrate how a real-world context can be used to develop outcomes in the Constructivist classroom.

CONSTRUCTIVIST ACTIVITY 1.2:
Making School "More Authentic"—Context

Description: The previous activity used the "real world" to find skills to embed into the school curriculum. A second method of embedding authenticity is to use newspaper, magazines, and newscasts to find real-world situations that involve the curriculum topic you wish to study.

For example, when I was teaching the topic of solving equations with the variable on both sides of the equation, I came upon a newspaper article that discussed how a large union and a manufacturing company were in difficult negotiations. The union wanted workers who were currently making nearly $28.00 an hour to cuts up to $18.50 an hour. After thinking about this, I realized that the equation $18.5x + 50,000 = 28x$ could be used to investigate this situation. I passed out the following handout, with the original article to the class.

HANDOUT

Attached is an article that our lesson is based on. You are the union rep, and you are to write a letter to your members recommending whether they should accept the offer of reducing their wage from $28 to $18.90 an hour or take the $50,000. In the letter you must provide and explain the algebra that was used to determine the recommendation.

Note: This authentic situation, like most, is messy, and a closer look indicates that there are many issues to consider, such as what is meant by "up to $50,000" and how long will the rate stay at $18.50? The concept of "messiness" will be discussed later in this book, but the point here is that authentic situations can be used to deliver the Constructivist philosophy.

2

An Introduction to Constructivist Teaching

In this chapter we provide background information on the Constructivist philosophy, discussing four points:

- What Constructivism really is.
- How this book will enable you to become a constructivist teacher.
- How Constructivist thought arose and evolved.
- Why it is important to study Constructivism.

2.1 What Is Constructivism?

Constructivism is actually a philosophy and theory and not pedagogy (Airasian & Walsh, 1997; Brooks & Brooks, 1993; Fosnot & Perry, 2005). The Constructivist philosophy is a description of knowledge rather than a prescription for learning. Airasian and Walsh wrote, "Although constructivism might provide a model of knowing and learning that could be useful for educational purposes, at present the constructivist model is descriptive, not prescriptive" (p. 444). Foote, Vermette, and Battaglia (2001) also view Con-

The Comprehensive Handbook of Constructivist Teaching, pages 7–28
Copyright © 2010 by Information Age Publishing
All rights of reproduction in any form reserved.

structivism as a descriptive entity: "Constructivism describes the processes undergone by the learner during instruction" (p. 3).

Many definitions of Constructivism have been proposed (Fosnot & Dolk, 2001; Gabler & Schroeder, 2003; Henson, 2004; Schwandt, 2003; Shapiro, 2002; von Glaserfeld, 2005), but they all adhere to the following characteristics:

- People of all ages do not discover knowledge; rather, they construct it or make it.
- People create knowledge by relating or connecting it to their previous knowledge.
- Knowledge is an autonomous and subjective construction.
- Learning involves active restructuring of how one thinks.
- People use personal experiences and social interaction to create knowledge; thus, one's learning and ability to learn are influenced by previous experiences.
- Cognitive growth is stimulated when people are confronted with practical, contextual problems or personal problems that present situations that require a new way to think.

Constructivism, then, is a philosophy that views knowledge as a subjective process that is shaped and structured by one's experiences. As a person encounters new experiences and situations, he connects these new experiences to previous knowledge bases and understandings. These connections not only add to the original knowledge base but also restructure that pre-existing knowledge base. A Constructivist teacher views his role as one of managing the learning environment and acting as guide, facilitator, and coach; the role of the Constructivist teacher is *not* one of transmitting knowledge.

2.2 Becoming a Constructivist Teacher

Reflecting on my own journey to becoming a Constructivist teacher brings back memories of the day my son was born. When the nurses put my son in my arms, I simultaneously felt joy and panic! While I was thrilled with having a son, I did not know what to do with him. I experienced this same reaction when I learned about Constructivist theory; I was excited to have a philosophy that described what I believed in, but I had no idea how to apply this philosophy. This book is intended to help you not only to get over that panic but also to develop concrete, observable teacher and student behaviors that will bring the Constructivist philosophy to life.

As you become a Constructivist teacher, you will find yourself thinking differently. You will think differently about how you think about knowledge, about learning, and about the role of the teacher. You will think differently about the planning process, the assessment process, and the curriculum. A Constructivist teacher thinks less about content and more about how to manage a class environment in which the learner interacts with materials and the world around him.

2.3   A Short History of Constructivist Thought

While individuals such as Dewey, Piaget, and Vygotsky are seen as Constructivists, they did not refer to themselves as such. It was not until the later part of the 20th century that the term was used in educational contexts. A search of descriptors in the ERIC database reveals that the earliest date that "Constructivism" was used as a descriptor was in 1977. Magoon used Constructivism in an article that he wrote for the *Review of Educational Research*. In that article, Magoon (1977) examined and outlined the use of the concept in the history and philosophy of social and behavioral sciences. His research included the field of education, and he found that "behavior like teaching and learning might be best understood as being constructed purposively by the subjects (both teachers and pupils)" (p. 652).

While the word "Constructivism" was not officially recognized by the education world until 1977, philosophers and educational writers, throughout the ages, have discussed the concept that individuals create their own knowledge through reflecting on their own concrete experiences and using these experiences to modify pre-existing knowledge. The following paragraphs provide a brief glimpse of the Constructivist movement throughout history. While not all the writers or philosophers cited are true or pure Constructivists, their writings contain portions of the philosophy.

2.3.1   *Ancient Writers*

Evidence of Constructivist thinking appears in the writings of several ancient philosophers. This evidence comes in the form of using prior knowledge and our senses to form new knowledge. The thinking of the ancient writers that follow indicates that in ancient times the notion already existed that knowledge is not transmitted, but rather is the result of a subjective process.

For example, Confucius presents some Constructivist views—although, arguably, his writings focus more on the interrelationship between learning and morality. Cooney, Cross, and Trunk (1993) quoted Section 2:11 from *Confucian Analects*: "When I have presented one corner of a subject to anyone, and he cannot from it learn the other three, I do not repeat my lesson" (p. 40). The reference by Confucius of learning from the other three corners aligns with the Constructivist characteristic of connecting to previous knowledge.

While Plato believed that human knowledge is not equal to absolute knowledge, he did acknowledge that people construct their own knowledge through their senses (Stevenson & Haberman, 1998). Their interpretation of Plato pointed to Constructivist characteristics:

> One thing that we can note immediately is that Plato realizes that human knowledge is not simply a matter of mere passive observation of things and events in the world around us. Our knowledge involves understanding, in that we actively interpret the data we receive through our sense organ, we apply concepts to classify and mentally organize what we perceive, using our rational powers. (Stevenson & Haberman, 1998, p. 92)

The phrases "actively interpret" and "classify and mentally organize what we perceive" are components of Constructivist thinking.

Aristotle believed, like Plato, that there is an absolute truth, but he allows for the human construction of knowledge. Taylor (1995) called attention to the fact that Aristotle believes that our senses help us understand absolute truth. He noted that Aristotle says we know things "as a result of induction from sense-experience" (p. 37) and noted that knowledge, in Aristotle's view, is consistent with the Constructivist characteristic of learning through the senses and experiences. Aristotle is expressing the Constructivist premise that one organizes his experiences with the environment.

2.3.2 *Medieval Writers*

The characteristics described previously in this chapter present knowledge as the product of an individual restructuring of their previous knowledge after experiencing new situations. The medieval writers presented in this section represent a course of thought that focuses on using prior knowledge, the senses, and personal experiences to create new knowledge. They thus represent a sampling of Constructivist thought.

Two Catholic theologians, St. Augustine and St. Thomas Aquinas, both present experience as a central component of learning. St. Augustine views the teacher not as one who transmits knowledge but as a person who manipulates the environment so one can learn (Reed & Johnson, 2000). St. Augustine not only envisions the role of the teacher as one who creates the learning environment but also views the creation of new knowledge as a process of using previous knowledge: "The Augustinian teacher believes that words become meaningful only to the extent that they can be connected with a set of experiences" (p. 31). St. Augustine voices the Constructivist philosophy when he views knowledge not as simply being transmitted but rather as the result of connecting the world to experience. The premise that one learns through personal experience implies the importance of using the senses to learn, and this certainly aligns with the Constructivist philosophy.

Though Thomas Aquinas is well known for his writings on theology, he also has contributed ideas and concepts regarding knowledge (Baggini & Stangroom, 2004). Aquinas' Constructivist traits come out by his "recognizing the central part played by sense perception in human cognition" (p. 22). Here Aquinas has acknowledged the role of one's senses in the construction of knowledge.

Vico advocated the subjective construction and context-oriented view of knowledge. Going against the trends of his time (Baggini & Stangroom, 2004), Vico did not believe that the natural sciences were the highest form of knowledge but felt that "truth may be achieved, but not by letting reason operate in the void: context is required" (p. 243). The word "context" indicates Vico's belief in the role personal experience plays in the construction of knowledge. Vico, by virtue of advocating context in achieving truth, is setting forth Constructivist principles. Vico's thinking is Constructivist in that it refers to "letting reason operate"; this is consistent with the Constructivist characteristic of restructuring one's thinking. Vico is also Constructivist when he describes context as a necessary element of learning.

One of the most influential philosophers of our time, John Locke, also presented Constructivist characteristics. Reed and Johnson (2000) describe Locke as not only attacking innate ideas but also presenting a "subsequent claim that all knowledge comes through the senses" (p. 53). Locke advocated the premise that reflection and the senses are the sources of ideas (Bentley, 1958). He believed that ideas are not innate (p. 60). One of his categories, complex ideas, is made "by an act of mind" (p. 60). The act of mind was broken down into three actions: combining simple ideas, relating two ideas, and abstracting from them real existence. Locke's belief that the senses are important to learning, and that the act of the mind involved the combining of ideas, directly flows into Constructivist characteristics.

Kant's view of knowledge is congruent to Plato's belief that there is an absolute knowledge that man cannot reach (Bentley, 1958). Kant, however, believed in "knowledge of phenomena, knowledge as it appears to our senses" (p. 72). Kant maintained that people construct their own ways of knowing the physical universe. While stipulating that there is a universal knowledge in physics and mathematics, Kant believed that "we can know only what we experience, that sensation forms the material of our knowledge" (p. 72).

2.3.3 Modern Writers

The modern writers examined here represent Constructivist thinking by viewing knowledge as the result of connecting previous experiences together and the importance of societal and contextual parameters. While some modern writers agree with the concept that knowledge is a process of subjectively constructing from previous knowledge, other writers take this idea one step further by stipulating that truth is constantly evolving as it reacts to a changing environment. Here we examine both these trains of thought.

Dewey (1991) stipulates that "successive portions of the reflective thought grow out of one another and support one another" (p. 3). Specifically, Dewey believed that knowledge is created by connecting to prior knowledge. Dewey is viewing knowledge as the product of recursive actions; in other words, knowledge grows from what is already known.

Piaget's theory is built on the premise that students learn by interpreting the results of their interactions with the environment (Fogarty, 1999). Specifically, "the learners' interactions lead to structural changes in how they think about something as they assimilate incoming data" (p. 76). The phrase "lead to structural changes" shows that Piaget viewed the modification of existing knowledge structures (previous knowledge) as a key element to knowledge creation. In distinguishing between different levels of thinking, Piaget (2001) states that one must examine "what must be added to sensori-motor intelligence for it to be extended into conceptual thought" (p.132). The phrases "added to" and "extended into" align with the Constructivist philosophy of constructing knowledge by restructuring previous knowledge.

William James extended the premise of using personal previous knowledge for knowledge construction to include the role of society. James (1991) viewed knowledge as an entity that is created by events, which is actually a process:

> The truth of an idea is not a stagnant property inherent in it. Truth happens to an idea. It becomes true, is made true by events. Its verity is in fact an event, a process: The process namely of its verifying itself, its verification. Its validity is the process of its validation. (p. 29)

This idea supported the Constructivist principle that truth or knowledge is context-related and is created as a result of interacting with the environment or solving problems inherent in the environment.

Richard Rorty is a modern philosopher whose ideas parallel those of James. He also claimed that truth is reliant on context and is ever-changing (Rorty, 1991). Rorty argued that "there is always room for improved belief, since new evidence or news hypotheses, or a whole new vocabulary, may come along" (p. 23). In other words, Rorty maintained that truth or knowledge is an ever-changing entity that adapts to events. The notion that man creates knowledge as a response to new situations aligns with the Constructivist philosophy of learning through experiences and restructuring prior knowledge.

We can gain further insight into the influence of social experience from Lev Vygotsky. Vygotsky wedded the concept of connecting to personal knowledge with that of the importance of contextual (societal) situations. Vygotsky claimed that knowledge or thought is a personal construction done within a social context (Popkewitz, 1998). Vygotsky believes that thought should be viewed "as an activity rather than as a passive, idealized process" (p. 538). Vygotsky's (1962) belief that knowledge is a continual personal construction is evidenced in his theory of spontaneous knowledge and scientific knowledge. Spontaneous knowledge is knowledge that the student constructs from his everyday experience, while scientific knowledge is knowledge that the student constructs through direct, formal instruction.

> We believe that the two processes—the development of spontaneous and of nonspontaneous concepts—are related and constantly influence each other. They are parts of a single process: the development of concept formation which is affected by varying external and internal conditions but is essentially a unitary process. (p. 85)

Vygotsky's view of spontaneous knowledge is representative of the Constructivist philosophy. By advocating the connecting of school and personal experiences, Vygotsky was stating his belief that knowledge is formed by the connecting of existing knowledge with new experiences. Fogarty (1999) stated that "Vygotsky's theory suggests that we learn first through person-to-person interactions" (p. 77). Learning through person-to-person interaction implies that one's opinion will change, and this idea aligns with the theories of Rorty and James.

Jensen (2006), a former teacher known for transmitting the findings of neuroscience into classroom practice, also included elements of the Constructivist philosophy in his writings, specifically the Constructivist belief that one's experiences and environment influence one's learning. He discussed a French study in which the files of adopted and abandoned children were identified. These students, between the ages of four and six, were initially tested before they went to live in new homes for 8 to 10 years. They were then retested, and the results indicated that there were significant gains in IQ. Arguably, socioeconomic status was a factor in this study. The lower the initial IQ, the greater the gain. Jensen discusses another project, the Abecedarian Project. In this study, infants from low-income families were randomly assigned to one of two groups. While both groups received nutritional support and medical care, the experimental group was given developmentally appropriate activities, games, enrichment learning, and emotional and social support. The experimental group consistently scored higher on mental tests through the age of 21, possessed enhanced language skills, consistently had higher reading achievement scores, had moderately higher mathematics achievement scores, and were more likely to still be in school at age 21. This study indicated that the environment in which a person interacts is a factor in the learning process and that the learning structure of the individual is influenced by the environment.

2.4   Influence of the Constructivist Philosophy

Although the word "Constructivism" has made its official appearance relatively recently, the preceding overview showed that the spirit of the philosophy has embedded itself throughout time. The fact that Constructivism or components of it have been a theme of influential writers indicates one aspect of the importance of studying Constructivism. In this section we expand on this idea.

2.4.1   Why Study Constructivism?

As a professional educator you will be asked many times to discuss your philosophy of education. In this day of high-stakes testing, your Constructivist philosophy will come under close scrutiny, and it will be important to justify your implementation of the Constructivist theory. The previous sections show that through the years the Constructivist philosophy has been advocated, implicitly or explicitly, as a philosophy that accurately describes how one learns. Michael Mahoney studied the use of "construct-based" terms during the period 1974–2002 and concluded that current trends indicate that Constructivism is increasing in its influence on society: "It is appearing with an accelerating frequency in titles of books and articles in psychology" (Mahoney, 2003, p. 1). Mahoney's research indicated that, in 1974, there were fewer than 1,000 instances of the use of "construct" words in titles and abstracts of psychological articles. His research also indicated that, in 2002, such words appeared more than 4,000 times. In the following we examine specific reasons for the increasing interest in the Constructivist philosophy.

2.4.2 Constructivism as an Umbrella Concept

The characteristics of Constructivism presented in Section 2.1 are shared by three highly regarded learning theories: brain-based learning, multiple intelligences, and differentiated learning. Since Constructivism has the characteristics of all three theories, Constructivism can be considered an umbrella concept. Let us examine this relationship more closely.

Brain-Based Learning

Wolfe (2001), Willis (2006), Connell (2005), and Jensen (1998), in their writings on how the brain learns, presented ideas that are congruent to the Constructivist philosophy. All three used Constructivism principles by stating that the brain changes itself by connecting different storage areas. Wolfe stated that students learn by recognizing patterns and "then make connections required to process the working memories so they can travel into the brain's long-term storage areas" (p. 6). The concept of processing working memories aligns with the Constructivist notion of restructuring prior knowledge and connecting prior knowledge with new experiences. Willis (2006), in discussing meaning and retention, stated that "information that fits into or adds to an existing network has a much better chance of storage than information that doesn't" (p. 103). The phrase "adds to an existing network" parallels the Constructivist characteristic of restructuring or modifying previous knowledge. Connell (2005), in discussing the physical change in the brain as one learns, stated, "As we grow and learn, the cells in our brain and nervous system connect in complex patterns of neural pathways" (p. 25). Jensen (1998) believed that the brain must make connections in order for us to learn, and he argued that these connections result in the rewiring of the brain: "Learning changes the brain because it can rewrite itself with each new stimulation, experience, and behavior" (p. 13).

Brain research supports the fact that knowledge is a subjective entity. Our brains may have the same components, but they are wired differently. Moreover, each learning experience compounds the uniqueness of a brain because "the more we learn, the more unique we become" (Caine & Caine, 1991, p. 87).

Multiple Intelligences and Multiple Skills and Domains

Consider this: While most of you would readily agree that a neurosurgeon may be one of the most intelligent people on earth, his intelligence is minimized on a blustery January midnight in Chicago when your car will not start. The surgeon's ability to perform dangerous surgery does not necessarily mean that he can get your car started. Gardner (1993) raised this point when he defined intelligence as the "ability to solve problems, or to fashion products, that are valued in one or more cultural or community settings" (p. 7). Gardner's notion that intelligence is defined by a context aligns with the Constructivist principle that people learn by working in a context of solving problems.

Fischer and Rose (1998) view learning and thinking as "changing in parallel along multiple strands or domains, as reflected in such concepts as Gardner's (1993) multiple intelligences" (p. 56). The concept of strands coincides with Wolfe's theory of sensory memory. The activation of different strands enables the learner to take in information through different senses. Wolfe (2001) wrote, "The role of the sensory memory is to take the information coming into the brain through the sensory receptors" (p. 78). Thus, Gardner's and Fischer and Rose's theories have a dual path to Constructivist theory.

Differentiated Instruction

What is differentiated instruction? Well, it certainly not a new concept (Anderson, 2007). Differentiated instruction, Anderson pointed out, "integrates what we know about constructivist learning theory, learning styles, and brain development" (p. 50). Differentiated instruction, more precisely, consists of a set of strategies that helps teachers meet the unique needs of each student in a diverse classroom (Levy, 2008). In discussing instruction, Tomlinson (1999) called for differentiating in terms of content, process, and product. Content refers to what is taught, process refers to how designing activities to ensure that all students use their particular strengths to learn, and product refers to the tools students use to demonstrate their learning.

Consider the case of solving equations. In terms of content, students who have not mastered the addition of signed numbers will not be ready for solving equations and thus must be given instruction in this area before they move on. A student who already has some knowledge of solving equations may not need basic instruction but may need instruction on solving more complex equations. Thus, students may be grouped in terms of their needs. It is the idea of readiness that can be used to differentiate in terms of content.

Differentiating by process involves analyzing how students learn. Levy (2008) offered insight into differentiating by process. While some students may learn by listening to the teacher (auditory learners), some students need to see things on the board (visual learners), and some students learn by discussion (verbal learners). Levy also pointed out that it is effective to group different types of learners together and that a teacher can group students in terms of their interests. The idea of learning styles structures differentiation by process.

Differentiating by products includes giving quizzes, open-notes tests, publisher-written tests, teacher-made tests, projects, performance and authentic assessments, and journal writing. The concepts of interests and preferences form the foundation for differentiating by product.

These ideas correlate with the Constructivist characteristics of knowledge and knowledge being contextual and knowledge being a subjective process of adding onto previous knowledge. The Constructivist characteristics of subjective knowledge creation being influenced by the environment naturally flows with differentiated instruction. Tomlinson (1998) expands on this theme by stating that "intelligence is multifaceted" and that "it is fluid, not fixed" (p. 18). She connected with the Constructivist premise of subjectivity when she said, "Each brain needs to make its own meaning of ideas and skills" (p. 54).

2.4.3   Constructivism and Academic Achievement

Constructivist teaching strategies have been shown to be effective at different levels of schooling. From early childhood education on and up through teacher education courses, the Constructivist method of teaching has been successful. Let us examine this situation in more detail.

The education community generally looks to the Constructivist community as providing a structure for organizing the curriculum. An example comes from the state of Missouri (Schattgen, 1997). The Missouri Department of Elementary and Secondary Education is using Constructivist theory and research to inform and shape educational policy and practice. Project Construct, an early childhood reform initiative that is designed to translate the theory of Piaget into practice, is an extended statewide effort to deliver the Constructivist philosophy to early childhood teachers. Project Construct has conducted a 30-hour institute that empowers participants to develop Constructivist practices. The Project Construct National Center also commissioned an independent study to examine the effects of different teaching strategies on kindergarten students. The study found that "students whose teachers engaged in practices that are consistent with constructivism attained higher levels of achievement than students whose teachers employed more traditional practices" (Schattgen, 1997, p. 37).

DeVries (2002) reported on several studies that have examined the effects of applying Constructivist methods in schools. For example, Morse's study on second- and third-grade students in Missouri. Morse reported that children educated through Constructivist curriculums scored at or above the national average in reading, mathematics, and total basic battery of the Stanford Achievement levels at the end of third grade. DeVries also discussed the study of Constance Kamii (2000) of first-grade children from a Constructivist classroom and traditional classroom. Kamii examined the children on word problems and computational problems. She reported that the Constructivist group did better than other groups on all 13-word problems and that their explanations showed better part-whole logic.

The DeVries report also analyzed Araujo's study examining the moral autonomy of school children from three preschool centers. In both 1992 and 1995 students from the Constructivist center expressed higher personal autonomy; in 1999, however, the Constructivist children scored lower. Araujo speculated that the other groups started to receive "values education" and that the Constructivist children were reaching a ceiling.

DeVries extended her analysis to include international studies. One of the studies she analyzed was that of Duckworth, who conducted a study under the authority of the Kenya Institute of Education. This study, extending over three years, involved children from 5 to 15 years of age and examined the complexity and diversity of their thinking. Students from the group taught by Constructivist methods demonstrated more complex thinking, and the group that were taught for the longest time using Constructivist methods (three years) did better than the group that was in the program the least.

DeVries extended the Duckworth project by analyzing the work done in Evanston, Illinois, kindergarten classes. Kindergarten students taught using a Constructivist approach were compared to students taught with traditional methods. Results indicate that the students taught by Constructivist methods showed more complex thinking.

A curriculum structured on a social Constructivist approach to literacy has been successful in increasing student scores (Au & Carroll, 1997). This approach was developed at the Kamehameha Elementary Education Program and was designed to improve the literacy achievement of Native Hawaiian students. The results were dramatic:

> After only 1 year in the project [the] first group of teachers was able to reverse student achievement for the writing process: 68% of students were now above or at grade level and only 32% were below. The same dramatic pattern held true for [the] second group of teachers. (p. 217)

Kim (2005) studied the effects of a Constructivist approach on elementary school children. This study was done in Korea during a period in which there was a paradigm shift in public education in Korea. The general public, including parents, criticized the public school system for not preparing Korean students for the information society that will appear in the 21st century; there was concern whether Korean students were trained to develop creative thinking and to effectively problem solve. This study analyzed the effects of both traditional teaching and Constructivist teaching in terms of academic achievement, self-concept, learning strategies, and student preference for teaching styles. A total of 76 sixth graders were divided into two groups. One group was taught with traditional methods. This method of teaching consisted of three steps: introduction, development, and review. The Constructivist teaching method consisted of five steps: inviting ideas, exploring, proposing, explanation and solution, and taking action. Two instruments drove the study: an academic achievement test made by the classroom teacher and a self-concept inventor. The results indicated that the Constructivist approach was more effective than the traditional approach in academic achievement, motivation, anxiety toward learning, and self-monitoring. This study also measured student preference for a teaching paradigm. Students completed an attitude scale after they had experienced the Constructivist teaching method. This attitude scale consisted of four parts. The first part measured student perception of enjoyment and the teacher's role. The second section measured the quality of instruction and student opinions about the instructor. The third section enabled students to give their opinions regarding what aspects of the instruction they perceived as positive and negative. The last section of the attitude scale provided the opportunity to choose a favored instructional method. Seventy-three percent of the students preferred the Constructivist method. The reasons for their preference included more student involvement, increased student motivation, and greater ease in understanding the concepts.

The Bill & Melinda Gates Foundation, in 2000, began an education initiative that focused on school reinvention in the state of Washington. The overall goal of this initiative was to improve the learning of all students. The Foundation provided a gift that resulted in the establishment of the Washington School Research Center (WSRC), an independent research and data analysis center within Seattle Pacific University. The mission of WSRC is to conduct research on the learning of students in the public school. During the 2001–2002 school year, a third-party evaluation team studied 34 schools to determine the degree to which Constructivist teaching was present in the schools. The study also examined the degree to which Constructivist teaching was effective. The design of the study was to provide a representative sample of classrooms from language arts, science, social science, and mathematics. The study then correlated the variables writing, reading, mathematics, low-income, and Constructivist teaching. The data indicated that low-income correlated negatively with all other variables but that Constructivist teaching correlated positively with all levels of achievement. Even more impressive was the data indicating that Constructivist teaching does predict student achievement beyond the effects of school-level family income.

Hubber (2005) examined a secondary school class studying geometric optics in which the teaching was structured by the Constructivist philosophy. This class was a science elective class that included both ninth and tenth grade students and implemented the Constructivist philosophy. A Likert-type preference inventory was administered to students toward the end of the teaching sequence. Additionally, six students were interviewed concerning their responses to the survey. The results of the study also indicated that students preferred small group discussions, practical or relevant work, activities that enable them to create and test their own ideas, and having fewer notes that they construct as opposed to having the teacher dictate notes to them. These are all Constructivist activities and indicate that the class in this study did employ the Constructivist philosophy. Hubber concluded, "The constructivist-informed teaching approaches that allowed for students to freely express their ideas and be involved in the activities represented a successful experience for both the teacher and the students" (p. 29).

Constructivist methods are effective not only at the elementary and secondary levels but also for vocational school students. In Thailand, behaviorism has been the learning theory used by vocational schools, but the public has begun to demand that the nation's public schools keep pace with the demands of the 21st century. Also, the National Educational Act for Thailand assures that each Thai citizen has the potential to learn and is at the center of class activities. This is the backdrop for a study done in Thailand by Becker and Maunsaiyat (2004). This study compared the effects of Constructivist teaching and traditional teaching on students studying electronics at two selected technical schools; it did this by comparing Constructivist teaching to traditional teaching. The study examined two research questions. A total of 108 students were in the sample, with two intact classes at each of the two schools being studied. A counterbalanced design was used, meaning that both classes received both treatments. The study examined two questions, with the first one looking at the students' knowledge of electronics and the second question focusing on student preference for teaching method. Results of the study found that students taught with Constructivist methods scored higher on posttests and the delayed posttest. Moreover, the students preferred Constructivist methods.

The positive effect of Constructivist methods is also seen at the collegiate and professional levels. Lord (1997) studied two large sections of a general biology course for nonmajors; the purpose of the study was to see whether teaching based on the Constructivist philosophy would influence the learning of students in a large setting when compared to students taught by traditional methods. While both sections were given the same information, one was taught with the teacher-centered manner, and the other was taught with the Constructivist format. This study measured the results in terms of scores on unit exams and on an assessment questionnaire. This questionnaire included topics such as course workload, course organization, instructor teaching effectiveness, and the difficulty and fairness of the course unit exams. At the end of the questionnaire students were encouraged to express their feelings and concerns about the way the course was taught. On unit exams the Constructivist group scored statistically higher on all four unit exams, outperforming the control group at a significance level of 0.05 or better. While both groups scored approximately the same on test items requiring lower-level thinking, the Constructivist group scored significantly higher on test items requiring more than rote memory. The results from the student evaluations brought other positive insights concerning the Constructivist method. The Constructivist group indicated that they believed the class to be enjoyable and challenging (85%), while a majority of students in the control group (58%) found the course to be difficult and demanding. Another strength of the Constructivist approach revealed by student comments was that of student understanding. Many students (72%) of the experimental group (Constructivist approach) indicated that the approach enabled them to understand the material.

Bacon and Bloom (1995) used a holistic Constructivist approach to reform graduate teacher education. Their approach was based on four principles:

1. Student work must be an individual endeavor, and it must be related to the students' professional development and previous experiences.
2. Student work addresses problems encountered by the students in their daily work as a teacher; these problems should include an audience beyond the teacher and the university.
3. Student work should be developed through a collaborative process with faculty and peers.
4. Evaluating student work should be a process of utilizing authentic products, self-reflection, and focus on learning from one's mistakes.

They implemented these four Constructivist principles in their graduate program in behavior disorders by developing a portfolio model of evaluation. The portfolio model of evaluation replaced the final master's comprehensive exam. The students completed a series of projects that were put into a portfolio. To describe how the process worked, Bacon and Bloom (1995) recorded conversations with three of the students. These conversations, along with subsequent changes by students in their own classrooms and their published work, indicate the effectiveness of Constructivist principles: "From their work, we are convinced that teacher education programs can be major contributors to school reform via the implementation of constructivist approaches" (p. 645).

Another example of using the Constructivist pedagogy at the professional level comes from the University of Washington. The education faculty there team-taught a two-quarter course titled, Adolescent Development and Education, that uses a Constructivist approach (Lownebraun & Nolen, 1998). In assessing the effectiveness of the Constructivist pedagogy, the study had students complete an anonymous student ratings scale. At the end of the two-quarter course students gave the course a rating of 4.9 on a scale of 5.0. This rating put the course in the ninth decile for both the College of Education and the university. In discussing the effectiveness of using Constructivist teaching Lowenbraun and Nolen believe that "this constructivist approach both enables our students to develop the skills they need to become lifelong learners in their chosen careers and models good teaching practice for them to use with their own students" (p. 10).

The Constructivist philosophy has also been effective in the arena of learning a second language. Wannagat (2007) examined the variables of teacher talk, student talk, and code switching in two different English learning environments: a content and language integrated Learning (CLIL) environment and an English as a medium of instruction environment. The study was based on data obtained from observations of history lessons in each environment. These observations were from videotaping, transcriptions, and a questionnaire administered to all students. There were also guided interviews with history teachers and selected students. In examining the different environments Wannagat used the parameters of speech distribution (percentage of teacher talk vs. student talk), length of student speech, and length of student utterances. In discussing the results of the study, Wannagat (2007) used the theories of Wolff, who "argues that language is learned because meaning is constructed; comprehension is not reactive and receptive, but it is a highly active, constructive process" (p. 678). In discussing the advantage of the CLIC environment, Wannagat stated, "It seems that an advantage of learning in the CLIL context is the increased opportunity for learners to develop their constructive abilities in L2" (p. 678).

2.4.4 Special and Diversified Learning Needs

Constructivism, as a curriculum organizer and as a teaching strategy, has been effective for diverse types of students, including those labeled as having special needs, students regarded as gifted, and students considered at-risk.

Georgeson, Gann, and Nourse (2003) discussed the diversity of classrooms in Washington State. Their article was intended for supervisors of student teachers to examine how to prepare their students for a diversified teaching environment. The authors noted that since the past 15–20 years have seen a change in the demographics of schools in the state, teachers in urban settings in the state will see a diversified student mix, including students who have limited English ability, low-income students, transient students, and "at-risk" students. The authors of this study believe that "this mix of students does not match well with one style of learning or a non-flexible system of educating children" (p. 3). They encouraged student teacher supervisors to "set appropriate timelines for teacher-preparedness, teach the tenets of a constructivist teaching philosophy" (p. 3). They concluded that "combining the tenets of 'constructivism' and the best practices described above can prepare successful new teachers and meet the unique needs of a diverse student body" (p .9).

The use of technology embedded in a Constructivist environment can be an aid to at-risk students. Pugalee (2001) reported a study examining a development algebra class whose students were classified as low math performers because they had received a D or F grade in a previous math class. The purpose of the study was to substantiate the usefulness of a Constructivist approach in teaching algebraic concepts to students who are typically left out of mainstream mathematics and to substantiate the usefulness of technology in the process; hence, graphics calculators were used in a Constructivist environment. Data, including student work and writing, was collected during a unit during the course. The data included student work and student writing. Data on the exam indicated that more than 86% of the students scored a C or better. Pugalee concluded that students became engaged in their own learning by exploring important concepts and making connections. He pointed to the importance of such results as "especially relevant because marginalized students validated the effectiveness of constructivist principles by generating a classroom environment that facilitated mathematical understanding" (p. 6). Pugalee also stated that "graphic calculators enabled the students in this study to explore relevant algebraic ideas through constructivist methods" (p. 6).

Moses, Klein, and Altman (2001) presented a case for using Constructivist teaching with individuals with learning disabilities. They examined an application of Piagetian cognitive theory to the assessment of adult language. Piaget's theories, which are Constructivist in nature, were successful in the scenario presented by Moses and his associates. They reasoned that one's linguistic performance can be enhanced by facilitating the ability to reason about causality and enhancing the ability to understand causal relationships; this can be done by clinician intervention. They argue that "the clinician's objective in intervention would be to help an individual engage in constructive activity and reconstruct selection, organization, and inference-making patterns in the process" (p. 223). The authors, in their concluding remarks, stated that "it would be beneficial for teachers to engage individuals with learning disabilities in constructive activity regardless of type or severity of the disorder" (p. 226).

Students who are labeled as gifted will also benefit from instruction the Constructivist theory. Graffam (2003) examined the positive effects of using the "teaching for understanding" (TfU) framework. Developed at Harvard's Project Zero, TfU "is a constructivist approach to the learning process" (p. 13). Not only is TfU a Constructivist teaching environment, it "is a perfect vehicle for gifted classrooms" (p. 13). Graffam, in discussing the TfU framework and how it is important for students to accept this paradigm, stated that "utilizing constructivist practices to introduce the framework to those who will be using it not only makes good pedagogical sense, it validates the concept of understanding itself" (p. 18).

Constructivism is also being used to restructure music education. Webster (2000) examined a redefinition of music education; this redefinition includes a music education curriculum that not only considers performance-based education reaching a small number of students but serves a wider base of students through composition, improvisation, and active listening. He advocated the use of music technology, the Internet, and "more divergent experiences that engage students' imaginations" (p. 7). He believed not only in a wider base of music education but also in "how we teach this content" (p. 4). Webster maintained that good teaching must structure music teaching environments that will enable students to engage in musical thinking. He advocated the use of Constructivism as the foundation of this rethinking: "Constructivism as a philosophy of education has much to teach us in music as we consider the design of more effective teaching strategies" (p. 5).

2.5 Constructivism as a Curricular Organizer for Adult and Professional Learners

The Constructivist philosophy not only translates into instructional strategies, it can also be seen as a philosophy or foundation for curriculum design. The curriculum may be in adult education, in medical and nursing education, and online teaching.

Older learners possess a learning profile different from that of younger learners (Spigner-Littles & Anderson, 1999). Older learners respond more effectively in learning environments in which information is shared between instructor and students; this is done when the older learners connect the new learning experience to their existing knowledge base and reconstruct their prior understandings in order to understand this new experience. According to Spigner-Littles and Anderson, adult learners will learn best in a Constructivist environment: "Our observations of older learners tend to support the constructivist learning theory in that we found knowledge to be developed internally, rather than simply transmitted by an instructor to a passive student" (p. 205). This article refers to Constructivist principles that "recognize that the learning process among older learners is most effective when new information is connected to and builds upon prior knowledge and real-life experience" (p. 206).

Kaufman (2003), writing for the British Medical Association, discussed how as teachers we usually teach the way we were taught. He discussed how it would be beneficial to use a set of principles that a medical school instructor can use. Kaufman discussed several learning theories, one of which is Constructivism, about which he said, "Constructivism has important implications for teaching and learning" (p. 214).

Peters (2000) discussed how today's curriculum is still content-driven and teacher-centered. He noted that this approach is not in accord, for example, with the background of many nursing students who are adults and bring considerable life experiences and knowledge bases to the classroom. There must be a pedagogy that "can build on this vast knowledge base" (p. 1). Peters believes that "Constructivist theory may offer a framework for this to occur more readily than more traditional educational frameworks" (p. 1). He presented the position that "adults as learners require open and empowering learning environments" (p. 6). What theory is congruent to this approach? Peters answered this question by stating that the Constructivist theory is "conducive to this approach, an approach that puts the focus of learning on the learners as constructors of knowledge rather than teachers as disseminators of knowledge" (p. 8).

The Constructivist philosophy is also structuring engineering education (Hansen, 2004; Porter, 1995). Porter discussed how ethics education in engineering classes faces a challenge: "Expecting an inexperienced student to grasp the full depth and breadth of ethical issues as they relate to specific case studies in the college classroom may be unreasonable" (p. 204). While a deep understanding of technology subjects develops relatively rapidly in the early stages of one's engineering studies, topics such as ethics, morals, and psychology develop at a slower pace. Porter discussed how the four-year apprenticeship, under the guidance of an experienced and practicing engineer, focuses on providing practical knowledge and knowledge of working with people. This is an ongoing process that extends a knowledge base into an effective practice. Porter (2004), while discussing what learning model can blend the formal learning process with the more informal learning, stated that "some combination of the constructivist learning model (CLM) and the behaviorist model (BLM) in the classroom may be appropriate, but for different applications" (p. 204). Constructivism, then, is the instrument for self-development and initiative for engineering students. Another example comes from a project-organized, problem-based learning curriculum in which engineering students learn by writing their own questions and finding their own answers (Hansen, 2004). When it came to the project assessment, however, the supervisor asked many of the questions. "From a constructivist point of view," Hansen stated, "this may seem inappropriate in relation to students' learning" (p. 1). For years at Aalborg, the norm was for students to answer questions asked by the teacher. To evaluate the effectiveness of this approach, Hansen conducted a participatory action research. Specifically, he used a new approach to assessment based on "operative constructivism" (p. 213). In this model the teacher perturbs student thinking in two ways. First, the student is required to ask question; second, the student and teacher participate in dialogue so the "student can gain the necessary feedback to construct a more complex meaning or understanding and in that way be able to answer the questions" (p. 215). Feedback indicated that most students agreed preferred this type of assessment compared with the traditional assessment (p. 219).

Online educators involved in distance education may also benefit from the use of a new pedagogy; the reason is that online learning is embedded in a different setting. Huang (2002) examined the impact of a Constructivist approach in online learning for adult learners. Advanced online technologies have advanced to the point that they have reduced barriers to interactive communications. Huang examined the connection between Constructivism and adult learning theory. He concluded that people designing distance education face the task of reflecting a shift in methodology and philosophy and that "Constructivist principles provide ideas to help instructors create learner-centered and collaborative environments" (p. 35).

2.6 Constructivism and the Global Economy in the 21st Century

The Constructivist philosophy is built around the belief that knowledge is the result of a subjective process that connects discrete pieces of knowledge to each other to create a new knowledge base. An examination of the thinking needed for the 21st century indicates the need to implement the Constructivist version of thinking.

Former Secretary of Labor Robert Reich (1992) claimed that the successful businessperson is one who can create and identify new problems: "The one true competitive advantage in skill is solving, identifying, and brokering new problems" (p. 184). One tool that Reich advocated is that of using, analyzing, and interpreting the tremendous amount of data that the information age has created: "Instead of emphasizing the transmission of information, the focus is on judgment and interpretation... The student learns to examine reality from many angles, in different lights, and thus to visualize new possibilities and choices" (p. 230).

Nidds and McGerald (1995), in discussing the politicization of education, stated that it is important to get views on educational change from a source free from political correctness and hidden agendas. They identified this group as corporate America. Corporate America knows the thinking skills needed by workers to make America competitive in a world market. Based on responses to questionnaires they had sent to CEOs of "Fortune 500" corporations, they concluded that "a majority of new workers lack... ability to apply their skills to new and unfamiliar problems, and ability to work effectively in groups" (pp. 27–28).

Urban cultural anthropologist Jennifer James, in discussing the type of intelligence needed to react to new, more complex patterns, stated that "the ability to understand, synthesize, and adapt to those patterns will become basic intelligence" (1996, p. 206).

In discussing the relationship between thinking and computer skills, Roman (2003) acknowledged that computers help the modern worker accomplish goals faster, but that is not enough to be successful on the job: "Today, I happen to use a computer as another tool to accomplish those goals, but I am still measured by my ability to think, create, and enrich" (p. 21). The Constructivist philosophy aligns with the words "create" and "enrich."

Mike Eskew (2006), chairman and CEO of UPS, said that he looks for "the ability to learn how to learn" (p. 7); this calls for individuals "who can manage complexity and uncertainty" (p. 7). The skills of analyzing information, managing uncertainty, integrating and synthesizing information, evaluating and applying knowledge to new situations, and learning how to learn all align with the Constructivist philosophy.

2.7   Constructivism, Psychotherapy, and Counseling

The Constructivist movement has found its way into psychotherapy and cognitive therapy (Favre & Bizzini, 1995; Mahoney, 1993; Neimeyer, 1993, 1995). Mahoney (1993) wrote: "This apparent growth in popularity may also be partially attributed to the fact that some of those writers portrayed as archetypal rationalists—Albert Ellis—have vigorously denied any rationalist leanings and laid strong claim to constructivist views" (p. 4). Niemeyer (1995) provided some rationale for the popularity of Constructivism in the field of psychotherapy, which he said "can be viewed as a kind of collaboration in the construction and reconstruction of meaning" (p. 3). Toomey and Ecker (2007) called for a framework that blends phenomenology with psychotherapy. They stated that "the conceptual framework of constructivism provides a particularly natural and compelling paradigm" (p. 203).

2.8   The Next Step

In this chapter we have focused on the formal foundations of Constructivism. The chapter is, therefore, filled with a wealth of references, far more than in the other chapters of this book. But you need not be overwhelmed by the treatment. Our intention is to show the wide applicability of Constructivist ideas to various levels of education and to various disciplines. Constructivism has a long history, dating from the ancient Greek philosophers, but for the 21st century it is playing an ever-increasing role. This chapter provides examples of how you can apply the formal theory to your work, whether in business or a technical profession or education. I have been a Constructivist for many years, and my excitement with the myriad possibilities Constructivism offers continues to grow. I hope in the remainder of this book to have you share with me some of this excitement.

3

Principles of Constructivism

This chapter examines the principles of Constructivism that I began formulating while I was a secondary-school teacher and then verified and reorganized through several years of research. These principles represent my *personal* version of Constructivism, but they may provide incentive for you to formulate your own principles, which you can then use in your own classrooms. The following paragraphs will take you through a condensed version of my own experience: First I'll present some exercises to help you create a specific principle, and then I'll provide research data and philosophical data to help verify and possibly restructure these principles.

3.1 How Does Knowledge Come into Existence?

As a young teacher I would often become frustrated with my students and would say to myself, "I can't believe they forgot that; I *told* them what to do." After years of such comments (to myself), I realized that I needed to examine just how knowledge comes into existence. The following paragraphs examine this question.

The Comprehensive Handbook of Constructivist Teaching, pages 29–42
Copyright © 2010 by Information Age Publishing
All rights of reproduction in any form reserved.

EXERCISE 3.1

In the space below please write about four or five sentences that:

1. Summarize what happened on September 11th,
2. State the implications this event has for America, and
3. Highlight how this as affected the presidency of George Bush.

I asked my wife and best friend to do the same exercise. Let's look at what my wife wrote:

1. Summarize what happened on September 11th
   Terrorists attacked the USA. Two planes were taken over by the terrorists; one flew into the Twin Towers, in New York City, and exploded, killing hundreds of innocent people. The other one was headed for Washington, DC. The second plane was diverted by passengers, but it still went down, killing everyone on board.

2. State the implications this event has for America
   Some say that the United States will never be the same. Patriotism became more apparent, many people flew the flag every day and it seemed that everyone supported our troops, our fireman, the police, and the government.

   Increased security is one of the most obvious changes. Racism and prejudice against third world people has increased.

3. Highlight how this has affected the presidency of George Bush
   Originally, the president was praised for his dealing with the chaos that followed. However, over time he has become the enemy, forcing his war on the nation. It seems that most people have lost respect for him.

Let's take a look at what another friend wrote:

I was home the day of the attack on the World Trade Center, I turned on my television at 9:00 A.M. and viewed the damage to one of the Towers, and it was shocking. The commentators spoke of the terrible accident that had just happened, and then the second aircraft hit the other Tower and reports that two other aircrafts had been hijacked and were feared to be on similar missions. I experienced feelings of great sorrow, dismay, and anxiety for the safety of our country. The events of that day proved that the USA was vulnerable to terrorist attacks, our defenses for that type of situation were inadequate, there were groups of people around the world, being shielded by certain nations, who irrationally hated America and wished to destroy our people and our way of life, our Constitutional Democratic Republic, and we needed to have a swift and effective military response to establish that our nation was strong and could defend itself.

Here is what I wrote:

On September 11th a group of terrorists attacked the United States. They did this in an "unconventional way" by hijacking commercial jetliners and flying them into the World Trade Towers. The events of September 11, 2001, made it clear that the military of the United States will be fighting a different type of war and a different type of enemy. Initially George Bush's presidency may have been given a boost because his initial response was well received. However, the perception is that his response, "The War on the Evil Axis," has been a failure.

It is obvious that not only was the format different, all three writings represent different interpretations of that event; both writers had their own version of their story.

Here is another example; look at the figure, which is my son's version of a famous optical illusion.

Figure 3.1

If you think that the point of this exercise is to have you create the principle that learning is a subjective and autonomous process, you are correct. Educators, researchers, philosophers, and cognitive scientists all verify this conclusion. Trotter (1995) discussed a situation in which a teacher asked a young student what "9 + 9" was. The teacher was surprised by the student's answer: "19." The student explained that, since 9 is 1 less than 10 and 10 + 10 is 20, 9 + 9 must be 19. Trotter explained the implications of this episode:

> [The teacher] was stunned because he saw in the imperfect reply a thought process that was "enormously robust for a 5-year old." The method was not one the child had been directly taught... rather, it was the child's own invention, which with refinements could lead toward powerful forms of mathematical reasoning. (p. 25)

The philosopher Thomas Dewey (1991) similarly noted that "thinking is specific, in that different things suggest their own appropriate meanings, tell their own unique stories, and in that they do this in very different ways with different persons" (p. 39). And brain researchers believe that although everyone has the "same set of systems, including our sense, and basic emotions, they are integrated differently in every brain" (Caine & Caine 1991).

Since every student is "wired differently," it is our duty as teachers to create a class environment in which students can create their own version of knowledge. This leads to Learning Principle 1:

Learning Principle 1: *Students learn by participating in activities that enable them to create their own version of knowledge. This includes creating their own rules, definitions, and experiments.*

3.2 How Do Students Remember?

Most teachers at one time or another have lamented, "Why don't my students remember anything?" The next exercise examines this question.

EXERCISE 3.2

Consider the activities the following students engaged in, and decide which one student will remember the most effectively. By effectively, I mean who remembered the most effectively. Be prepared to explain your answer.

- Student A takes very limited notes and decides just to try to remember as much as possible.
- Student B reads the chapter, underlines the main points, looks these over, and then says them aloud (to herself).
- Student C underlines the main points and then calls his friend up on the phone to discuss his ideas.
- Student D reads the chapter, writes out the main points, puts these ideas into a graphical organizer such as a web diagram, and uses these as she explains the concept when the teacher calls on her.

Most probably you stated that student D remembered the most effectively and the longest because she had to explain her ideas; similarly, you might have picked student C as a close second because he discussed his work with someone else. In all four cases, the students did more than simply listen, but the learning processes of the last two students were more active: they involved reaching out beyond oneself. Sosa (2006) would agree with you, citing research indicating that people remember more when they explain to someone else or teach someone else. He stated that the teaching someone is the most effective way to learn, or "in other words, whoever explains, learns" (p. 95). This idea leads to Learning Principle 2.

> **Learning Principle 2:** *Students learn when they teach others, explain to others, or demonstrate a concept to others.*

The activities of explaining to others and teaching others can be considered a performance, or *authentic,* activity. Newmann, Bryk, and Nagaoka (2001) used the term "authentic intellectual work" to describe the type of activity that enables one to learn. They argued that authentic intellectual work has a prior knowledge base, contains in-depth understanding such that relationships are created and tested, and involves elaborated communication. Elaborated communication is based on the concept that adults who work in the "real world" use "verbal, symbolic, and visual" (p. 15) tools to conduct their work. Their study demonstrated that "authentic intellectual assignments enrich instruction not only for able children, but for all students" (p. 27). Learning Principle 3 is the result of blending the concepts of in-depth understanding and elaborated communication.

> **Learning Principle 3:** *Students learn when they create products from the real world that involve narratives, explanations, justifications, and dialogue.*

3.3 What Does Knowledge Look Like?—Part 1

If we expect our students to demonstrate intelligence, then what are we exactly looking for? The next exercise and the following paragraphs will help you decide what it is you are looking for in your students.

EXERCISE 3.3

Think of the most intelligent person in your high school class, college class, or work. Write down your answer. Now, consider the following situation.

You are stranded on a deserted island, and your plane has disintegrated. In the crash your radios, cell phones, and other amenities were destroyed. One of the survivors is the person you defined as being the most intelligent. As you begin to talk with your friend about what to do, a person in a canoe signals you to get in his boat. He appears to be a local inhabitant; and as he wends his way to an inhabited island, he navigates by using the stars. Now, who is the most intelligent person you know?

Let's look at another situation.

Suppose it is 1:00 a.m. and you are stranded, and the temperature is −15°F. Suppose that a car mechanic, who dropped out of high school, happens to come by. Now, who is the most intelligent person that you know?

This exercise indicates that intelligence is context-specific and that it comes in different forms. Gardner (1993) listed the characteristics of intelligence, and among these characteristics is the ability to create products or solve a problem that is valuable in society. Gardner distinguished between intelligence and a "domain," a set of specific skills, questions, and symbolic systems. In contemporary society, algebra, geometry, rap music, and cooking are considered domains, while intelligence is a skill to solve a problem that is valued in a societal setting and *uses that domain.* As an example, surgeons, lawyers, and sports agents have different types of authentic (real-world) problems to solve. A surgeon must prepare for surgery, oversee his surgical team, perform the surgery, write up his report on the surgery, and then explain the process to the family members. A lawyer must write a brief, select a jury, and argue his case before a jury. A sports agent must analyze numbers, make decisions based on these numbers, and confer with parties who possess different perspectives. These activities certainly differ and represent different types of thinking processes. The key point is that intelligence comes in many forms. This is important for the Constructivist teacher who wishes to create an environment in which students create their own version of knowledge. Since knowledge, as this paragraph has demonstrated, is dictated by different contexts, the teacher must be cognizant of what form of knowledge the student is expected to create in society.

A question naturally arises: Is intelligence a general ability, or is it context-specific? Eric Jensen (2006) recounts the story of American psychologists who were alerted to the fact that Brazilian youngsters with no formal math were doing fast math with 98 to 99 percent accuracy; this was done as a part of business transactions as street merchants. Yet in a laboratory setting their accuracy dropped to half that rate, even for tasks that required the same "street" skills. According to Jensen, this result confirmed that "skills are highly context-dependent, not that the learners lack any general cognitive capacity" (p. 20).

I have had the privilege to work with students who were in Honors English courses and scored well on the writing portion of the ACT but struggled with drawing or interpreting diagrams. This situation might seem familiar to you: it sounds like the typical visual vs. verbal learning, or right brain vs. left brain. Case (1991) explained it differently, noting that cognitive structures are "assembled independently of each other structure" (p. 17). An analysis by Fischer and Rose (1998) reached a similar conclusion: "Unlike height, however, cognitive spurts are evident only under optimal support conditions, not across the entire array of children's behaviors" (p. 57). In other words, the development of cognitive skills is not consistent or linear. Hence, the Constructivist teacher must create an environment in which students are given the opportunity to develop each intelligence or domain. We cannot expect all skills to manifest themselves at the same time.

> **Learning Principle 4:** *Knowledge comes in multiple forms, and its development is not uniform; hence, students must be given the opportunity to develop each intelligence or domain.*

Learning Principle 4 raises a question: How can a teacher present lessons that can help develop diverse skills? Many researchers agree that learning and memory start with the senses. For example, Wolfe (2001) stated that "the role of sensory memory is to take the information coming into the brain through the sensory receptors" (p. 78). Accordingly, Judy Willis (2006) advocated using "multiple learning pathways such as several senses (hearing seeing, touching)" (p. 5). Learning Principle 5 addresses this concept.

> **Learning Principle 5:** *Students learn when class activities stimulate multiple senses.*

3.4   What Does Knowledge Look Like?—Part 2

EXERCISE 3.4

Consider the following situation.

> *You tell a class of students to solve the following equation: $3 \times -4 = 11$. Student A gets the correct answer and admits to just using trial and error to plug in the correct answer. Student B solves it by looking at a similar example on the board. Student C*

solves it on his own by showing all of his work. Student D solves it manually and then solves it using a graphing calculator. Student E does the same thing independently and then writes a short essay comparing and contrasting the two methods. (yes, this is far-fetched, but let's just look at it hypothetically). Which one knows about solving equations?

The answer is that they all do, at least to some extent. This exercise shows that knowledge can be measured by its complexity and level of abstraction. Cognitive scientists present views that support this. Diamond and Hopson (1998) created a model of how brain cells migrate in the brain. Diamond and Hopson envisioned neurons and cells migrating up vertical stems. In this model cells form different layers at different levels of the stem. Diamond and Hopson acknowledged the existence of these different levels when they wrote, "The cells migrate along the guide cells and at the right point, hop off and form a layer. Then the next group comes up and migrates right through this existing layer and forms a new one above it" (p. 44). The question that naturally arises is this: Do the different levels of neurons represent a different level of thinking? Diamond and Hopson believed that this is the case. They discussed the work of Arnold Scheibel, whose research focused on the correlation between brain structure and what we do in life:

> The team found that the higher a person's educational level, the more fourth-, fifth-, and sixth-order branching they could observe and document in the dendritic trees. Perhaps, their data suggest, by learning and using more words and complex ideas, the more highly educated person stimulates Wernicke's area dendrites to grow and branch. (p. 34)

How does a Constructivist educator represent this hierarchy? As a tool that describes the level of complexity of one's thinking, we can use Bloom's Taxonomy, which follows:

- Evaluation;
- Synthesis;
- Analysis;
- Application;
- Comprehension;
- Knowledge.

Sosa (2006) provided another model. He presents a model that modifies Bloom's original model. He suggested that the new model suggests a more fluid approach to describing the cognitive complexity of one's thinking. The revised model is below.

- Create;
- Evaluate;
- Analyze;
- Apply;
- Understand;
- Remember.

An examination of the two models shows that the second model uses verbs to describe each level of thinking and that Evaluate has been replaced by Create at the top level. While the exact model that the teacher chooses is not as important as the fact the teacher uses a tool for measuring knowledge, the category of "create" is important for the Constructivist educator because:

Learning Principle 6: *A student learns by creating knowledge at different levels of complexity and thinking.*

3.5 How Exactly Does Knowledge Come into Existence?

If knowledge is a subjective construction, then what are the nuts and bolts of creating knowledge? What does the brain do to create knowledge? The exercises below will enable you to develop a principle related to this concept.

EXERCISE 3.5

Look at this figure, and state what number it is.

Figure 3.2

Now, state what letter you see.

Let's do another activity that will use the same principle as above. Write out the names of as many states as you can in two minutes.

In the first case you were able to get both answers. The figure did not change. But once you were asked to name the number, you were able to connect to your scheme of number knowledge. The same principle applied when you were asked to name the letter. While the figure did not change, you were able to access your previous knowledge concerning letters and connect the new information to this.

In the second case, you were able to name the states by connecting this task to a mental scheme that you already possess. You may have started at the state of Washington and then worked your way down the coast. The important point is that you connected your previous knowledge of the states to this new experience. It is the concept of *connectedness* that is important. Wolfe (2001) depicted the "connecting process" as a "multifaceted, complex process that involves activating a large number of neural circuits in many areas of the brain" (p. 92). Knowledge, therefore, is not a single entity; rather it is a network of connections.

Learning Principle 7: *A student learns by connecting new experiences with existing knowledge or connecting previously discrete experiences to each other.*

3.6   What Does "Connecting" Look Like in the Classroom?

What does the actual process of connecting new experiences with existing sound and look like in the classroom? The following exercise and paragraphs examine this question.

EXERCISE 3.6

Write down the first things that come to your mind when I say "Alaska."

Now go to a travel book or the Internet and look at the modern hotels and buildings in Alaska; these new images force one to rethink or restructure one's concept of "Alaska." Foote, Vermette, and Battaglia (2001) referred to such a process as a "constant cycle of editing and revising, crafting and reformulating theories about how the world functions" (p. 20). Dolk, Uttenbogaard, and Fosnot (1997) hypothesize that this restructuring is a "developmental process of conceptual reorganization resulting from interactions between the learner and the environment" (p. 3). Marzano (2007) concluded that the "biggest effect involved activities designed to produce cognitive dissonance—discrepancies between what students believed to be accurate and what is presented as accurate" (p. 89). Learning Principle 8 summarizes these ideas.

> **Learning Principle 8:** *Students learn when they are continuously presented with problems, questions, or situations that force them to think differently.*

As students start the process of "thinking differently," one must ponder what concrete student behaviors result in the restructuring of knowledge and the connecting of previously discrete experiences. What will a person see and hear when he visits a classroom where students are making such connections? Wolfe (2001) discussed the concept of "elaborative rehearsal" and stated that this process "requires students to reflect on the information being taught, relate it to something they already know, form meaningful mental associations" (p. 129). Nuthall (1999) proposed the use of "multiple representations of the same experiences" (p. 326). By creating new mental associations, the student is building a new and different representation of what they know. While previous principles state that knowledge comes in different forms, Nuthall proposed that students learn when they are given the opportunity to form new mental networks; these new mental networks represent a different way of thinking about what they already know. Nuthall also recommended the use of narrative and interactive activities such as group work. Willis (2006) endorsed activating multiple senses, looking for patterns, connecting the school experience to the student's outside experience, creating an authentic product, and interpreting the material. Marzano (2007) examined comparing/contrasting, hypothesizing, summarizing, and using nonlinguistic representation as effective modes of teaching. Blending these ideas with our previous principles results in Learning Principle 9.

> **Learning Principle 9:** *Students learn by making connections through the "Standard Six": compare and contrast, hypothesize and predict, express understanding in multiple modes, find patterns, summarize, and find personal relevance.*

3.7   A Closer Look at the Role of the Mind

The previous nine principles address how the mind creates new knowledge by imposing order and new thinking structures on student experiences. There exists another function of the mind that involves knowledge construction. Have you noticed that when you are confronted with a difficult or novel situation, you often talk to yourself about it or talk out loud? This self-conversation represents our mind's ability to regulate itself and is known as "metacognition." Hall (2001) discussed some of the aspects of metacognition. Among these are knowing the limits of one's learning ability, knowing what learning tasks can be accomplished within a certain amount of time, and planning. Tobias (1994), an educator and parent, noted that there are different learning styles and that an individual has the capability to analyze his knowledge style. A proponent for analyzing learning styles and preferences, she maintained that "learning how to recognize and appreciate learning styles can help you identify the natural strengths and tendencies each individual possesses" (p. 9). Costa (1984) discussed self-monitoring skills such as knowing when a subgoal has been attained, detecting and predicting errors, and choosing appropriate strategies. These components of self-regulation can be combined to form Learning Principle 10.

Learning Principle 10: *A student regulates his learning by (1) knowing his own ability and learning style preference, (2) analyzing tasks and appropriate strategies, (3) choosing and analyzing appropriate goals, (4) analyzing and appraising his individual level of performance, and (5) managing his time effectively.*

3.8   Social Aspects of Learning

While much of the previous discussion has been on the individual construction of knowledge, we now examine the social aspects of knowledge construction.

There are actually two sets of actions. One set involves the interaction between two people. Another person may bring up apparent contradictions, another method, or another perspective, or may confirm the validity of a concept (Gallimore & Tharp, 1990; Hardy, 1997).

Vygotsky (1962) took this idea one step further. His version of social interaction is analogous to a small child trying to see over a large wall. When an adult picks the child up, the child can see over the wall. Vygotsky took a detailed look at the interaction between two people through his concept of the zone of proximal development (ZPD). He defined ZPD as the difference between what a student can do independently and what he can do with the assistance of an adult or a more capable peer. Just as the child can see over the wall with a little help, the ZPD defines intelligence as the ability to accomplish cognitive tasks with the help of a more capable peer or teacher.

The second societal contribution to knowledge construction is that of transmitting those skills important for participation in society. One school of thought asserts that as society changes, the skills that it deems important change, and in turn the definition of intelligence will change. Kornhaber and Krechevsky (1993), compared the definition of intelligence for an agrarian society with that for an industrial society. In an agrarian society, intelligence involves the ability to maintain social ties. It makes sense, then, that those who can secure such cooperation are said to be intelligent. In an industrialized society, however, survival depends on different skills; large portions of the society are not engaged in the production of food. This type of society develops a wide range of occupations that come from and need technological knowledge. The demand for new inventions and the increased complexity of finance, distribution, and other fields require a literate populace. Literacy is a necessary tool if one (or even a whole society) is to use science, mathematics, or other fields of study. Kornhaber and Krechevsky summarized this view: "All definitions of intelligence are shaped by the time, place and culture in which they evolve" (p. 231). Not only does society provide interactions with others that influence learning, but it also presents the skills that are necessary to participate in society. The skills needed in the 21st century are discussed in Chapter 2 and are captured in Learning Principles 2, 3, and 4. Learning Principles 11 and 12 describe the social aspects of learning.

Learning Principle 11:   *Students learn by working with other people who are the source of contradiction, different perspectives, and confirmation.*

Learning Principle 12:   *Modern society provides the source of authentic products for students to produce.*

3.9   Summary of the Principles

This chapter has focused on the Constructivist philosophy that knowledge is not transmitted to a person; rather, it is a personal construction. Using this as a starting point, we then examined six questions:

1. How does knowledge come into existence?
2. How do students remember?
3. What does knowledge look like?
4. How exactly does knowledge come into existence?
5. What does "connecting" look like?
6. What are the social aspects of learning?

Our examination led to the development of twelve "learning principles."
The next step in the process is to translate these principles into easy-to-
remember strategies for the teacher.

Our Constructivist journey can be described by the following diagram.

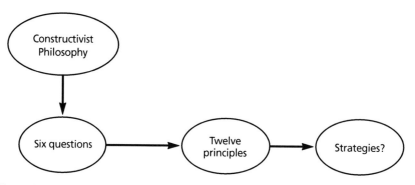

Figure 3.3

4

Translating Principles into Strategies

We are now ready to rework the 10 Learning Principles into a format that you can easily and immediately incorporate into your classroom practice.

4.1   A Closer Look at Learning Principles 1 and 2

An examination of Learning Principles 1 and 2 indicate that there exists a common theme. That theme is *autonomy*. In creating their own knowledge, by devising creating their own definitions, diagrams, summaries, and graphical organizers, students are showing autonomy. A metaphor for this is "Be the captain of your own ship." As a constructivist teacher you must constantly ask yourself, "Are my students captains of their own ship?" Learning Principle 10 expands on this point by extending autonomy to having the students work with others and explain their knowledge to others. Learning Principle 11 focuses on the concept of students creating their own knowledge by examining and critiquing their learning and their learning process. Blending Learning Principles 1, 2, 10, and 11 results in the learning strategy shown.

The Comprehensive Handbook of Constructivist Teaching, pages 43–47

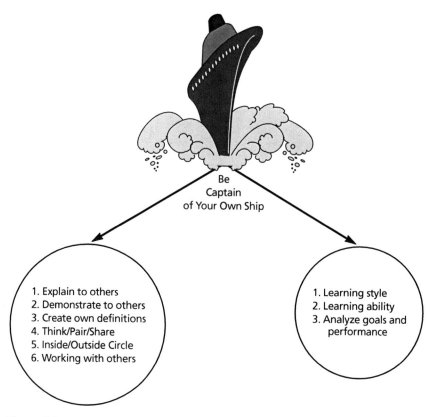

Figure 4.1

4.2 Extending the Concept of Autonomy

Definitions, demonstrations, and explanations are examples of authentic products, but a close look at Learning Principles 3, 4, and 12 bring a new parameter of authenticity into the mix. While explaining to a fellow student how to find the area of an irregular-shaped plot of land is "authentic," it is not the same as creating a bid for a millionaire house owner who wishes to put new sod in his lawn. While getting up in front of the class, doing a problem on the board, and explaining it is "authentic," it is not quite as authentic as putting your explanation in the form of a PowerPoint presentation or a letter or email. Explaining the steps and procedures in front of the class is "authentic," but doing so with the aid of a flowchart for a business meeting is another matter. Blending Learning Principles 3, 4, and 12 brings into our mix the concept of the real-world context and jobs. The mixing of real-world context and real-world tools results in a new metaphor and strategy: "Produce a reality TV show." Refer to the figure.

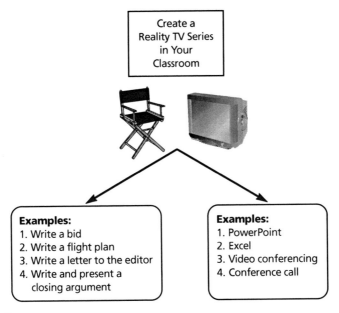

Figure 4.2

4.3 Creating a Learning Strategy for the Learning Process

Up to now the discussion has centered on general behaviors of learning and the products that demonstrate that learning. Blending Learning Principles 5, 6, 7, and 9 results in a learning strategy that depicts the actual mechanics of the learning process. As these principles have shown, the learning process begins with the senses and consists of connecting the discrete storage places of our understandings. Every time our brain connects two previously disconnected experiences, a new network of our knowledge appears. Each new connection or representation is a new picture of our learning schemes; the more we connect different experiences, the more new pictures of our learning appear. Every time a student compares discrete ideas, makes a prediction, finds a pattern, puts his understanding in the visual mode, finds his solution to a messy problem, or creates a summary of what he has learned, a new picture of his understanding is created. A metaphor that describes this situation is the kaleidoscope; each turn forms a new picture.

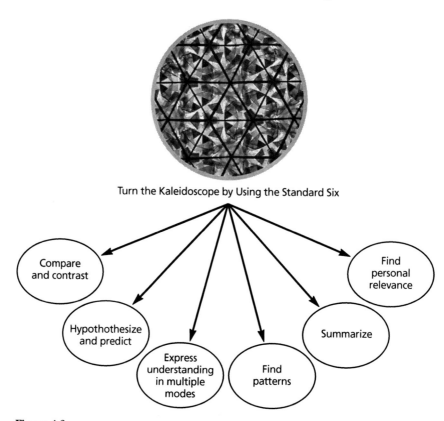

Turn the Kaleidoscope by Using the Standard Six

Figure 4.3

4.4 Another Look at the Learning Process

A closer look at the previous learning strategy indicates one area of the learning process that remains to be addressed: presenting a situation that the current thinking of the student cannot solve. The student must create a new knowledge scheme. In Piagetian terms, this is called creating "disequilibrium." In popular jargon this is what is called "Rattling the cage." By creating disequilibrium you can engage the learner to create a new learning strategy where the present one is ineffective. Learning Principle 8 addresses this situation and, when blended with the concept of the value of social interaction that is embedded through the principles, results in the following strategy, which is called "Rattling their cage." See Figure 4.4.

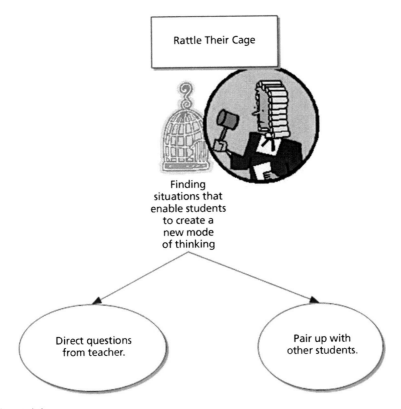

Figure 4.4

The "rattling of student cages" must be ongoing throughout the class. It is an integral part of the other strategies.

4.5 Creating a Creative Environment

These four easy-to-remember strategies will help the teacher create an environment in which students continuously create their own definitions, produce their own demonstrations, work in groups, express their learning in different modes, learn through their senses, formulate new thinking patterns as they experience novel situations, and produce authentic real-world products. By applying these four strategies, you will transform the classroom into a Constructivist class.

5

Creating a Constructivist Environment through the Linguistic Mode and Cooperative Learning

Consider this scenario. You get up in the morning, read the paper, and make a note to yourself concerning what to buy at the store after work. You then go to a local car dealership to get your car fixed and engage in our conversation with the mechanic concerning the problem. Next you go to the doctor's office for and explain to the doctor what physical ailments you are experiencing. You drive to work and conduct a business meeting. You work with your associates and have a discussion on the plan for a project. You type this out on a computer and pass out this plan. Your colleagues read this plan, a discussion follows, and parts of the plan are rephrased. A few minutes later you get a call from a German client in Berlin who has some questions for you. Since her English is not very effective and your German is also weak, you work very diligently to find the words that match her English vocabulary. Before you leave work, you check your email and respond to five emails. As this scenario indicates, we use language to function in everyday

The Comprehensive Handbook of Constructivist Teaching, pages 49–61
Copyright © 2010 by Information Age Publishing

life. We read the written word; we explain our thoughts to others through the spoken word and written word. We ask questions, we choose our words in order to connect with someone else who thinks differently from us, and we rewrite different documents. The key point concerning the *linguistic mode* is that language is a Constructivist activity. Think about this: how many times have you said something like "I know what I want to say, but I just cannot find the words to express it?" Fauconnier (1997) noted that language is a constructivist process: "Mappings between domains are at the heart of the unique human cognitive faculty of producing, transferring and processing meaning" (p.1). Fauconnier expanded on this idea when he wrote, "Meaning construction refers to the high-level, complex mental operations that apply within and across domains when we think, act, or communicate" (p. 1). Harvey and Goudvis (2007), in their book on teaching students how to read for understanding and comprehension, stated that strategic readers try to "better understand the text through their connections to the characters, the events, and the issues" (p. 12) The phrase "through their connections" illustrates the Constructive side of language development. The linguistic mode, essential to our everyday life, consists of talking with and explaining to others and writing our thoughts, and the thoughts of others, down in authentic documents. One must construct thoughts and ideas and then construct the words to convey those ideas. When the person we are communicating with does not connect with our words, we must construct new words and phrases in order to connect with that person. Levine (2002), a leading learning expert, reminded parents that they "should be aware that language is all-consuming in the everyday existence of their children. Obviously, it is the medium for communication with friends, siblings, teachers, pets, and parents" (pp. 120–121).

Our discussion of how a Constructivist teacher uses the linguistic mode can be broken into three components:

1. Cooperative learning.
2. Questioning.
3. Authentic writing.

This chapter examines cooperative learning, while Chapter 6 examines questioning and Chapter 7 focuses on authentic writing.

5.1 Cooperative Learning

Cooperative learning has different definitions, but it can be defined as a strategy in which a small, heterogeneous group of students share knowledge, complete projects or assignments, or master a body of knowledge (Vermette, 1998). What follows is an example of cooperative learning from an Assessment Measures class.

> The teacher has formed the students into groups of two. The teacher tells the class to write down the first few things that come to their mind when he says *"standardized tests."* The students write down their thoughts, and then the teacher tells the designated first person in each group that they have 30 seconds to present and explain their thoughts to their partner. Then the students switch roles. The teacher allows both students to summarize what they believe the other had said. The teacher follows this by calling on people to go to the board and write out what they learned from their partner concerning standardized tests.

This example illustrates some characteristics of cooperative learning. While cooperative learning has many forms, all the forms contain essential characteristics. There are five characteristics (Bowen, 2000; Doolittle, 1997) that can be used to define cooperative learning.

1. Positive interdependence: The characteristic of interdependence consists of giving tasks to students that can be completed only if all group members contribute; it involves the attainment of personal and group goals, the interdependence of roles, the interdependence of resources, and reward interdependence.
2. Face-to-face interaction: This characteristic involves each group member encouraging and facilitating other group members, providing feedback to each other, exchanging ideas and resources, and modifying each other's understanding.
3. Individual accountability: This characteristic involves all students accountable for their own work. This includes being accountable for the assessing what new knowledge they have created.
4. Interpersonal skills: While working with others to modify and expand each other's knowledge base, students are learning to share ideas, resolve apparent cognitive disconnects, and resolve all personal conflicts.
5. Group processing: Here students are given time to reflect on the processes and outcomes that took place in their group. This includes how the process enabled them to create new knowledge, what they learned about interacting with others, and how they would modify the process in the future.

Cooperative learning has a solid theoretical and pragmatic base from which to work, and research has shown that it is an effective teaching theory. A key component to cooperative learning is Vygotsky's Zone of Proximal Development (Doolittle, 1997, p. 88). Vygotsky envisioned one's cognitive level of development as described by a range of behaviors. At one end of this range is what the individual can learn with assistance from another; at the other end is learning that can occur independently. Vygotsky's ZPD is a continuum characterized by the level of independence exhibited at each stage. It is part of a recursive loop in which the learner needs assistance from more capable others, assists himself, internalizes and automates the knowledge, and then starts the cycle over. For Vygotsky, performance capacity is a progression through different levels of independence. See Figure 5.1.

Learning with assistance
from another

Learning
independent

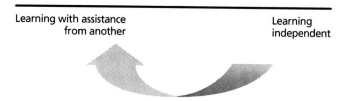

Figure 5.1

In an environment structured by cooperative learning (and the Zone of Proximal Development), students are exposed to a Constructivist environment. Let's look at one of the examples of cooperative learning from the first chapter.

> A group of high-school geometry students walk into a classroom and look at the screen in the front of the room. At each desk is a copy of a letter from a lawyer stating that in the recent lawsuit they filed, the defendant has come up with two possible settlements. One is to acquire the irregularly shaped parcel of land (shown on the overhead) which can then be sold for $1,500 an acre. The second settlement is to just take $350,000. After going over the letter and the diagram of the parcel of land, the teacher gets students into groups of two, and has the students discuss what they must know in order to solve this situation. One student discusses his answer for 30 seconds. Then they switch roles. The teacher then asks students to come to the board and write down what they learned from their partner.

Here the first student listening is learning new ideas from the first student talking. The student talking is assisting the listener in understanding his ideas. The time given to summarize their ideas represents movement along the continuum; the listener is internalizing new ideas (the ideas of the partner) and, by having the partner confirm the ideas on the board, has internalized new ideas and knowledge.

Below is another example of cooperative learning from the first chapter.

> Students are told that they will review the topic they just studied, and that there will be a test on it in two days. The teacher gets students in groups of two to create a Manual entitled "(Topic that they are studying) . . . for Dummies." The teacher tells the class that they are to use their imagination on this and to create what they would consider as the ideal study aid. The students are told that they can use this for the test. The teacher continuously goes throughout the room, and when he observes that all groups are on their way to developing the manual, he announces "have one partner go to the next group and learn what that group is doing." The "rover" goes back to his group and discusses what he has learned, and how his group could use these ideas in their manual. The teacher then tells the other partner to rotate two places, and replicate the same action as before. At the end of the "Dummies Manual activity," students are asked to write about the following prompts: What did you learn about x from this project? What did you learn about a non-topic (problem solving, working with another, etc.?)

This example of cooperative learning also follows the structure of the Zone of Proximal Development. The student who is a rover does not know what the people in the new group know, but starts the process of understanding by listening to the other people explain their ideas. The rover will ask questions of the new group members to help him learn, and may still need some coaching, but eventually will be able to explain the others' ideas independently. The rover then goes back to his original group and explains to his original group the ideas of the other group. It must be noted that there is a problem here, and that being that the rover still may not totally understand. It is the role and responsibility of the teacher to ensure that there is comprehensive understanding. The teacher may need to go throughout the room and monitor groups; the teacher may instruct members of the new group to coach the rover by having him repeat to them what they learned. The teacher may also have rovers go to the board and write on the board and explain what they learned from others. The important point is that the Zone of Proximal Development is a construct that frames cooperative learning.

Cooperative learning is a tool for delivering the Constructivist philosophy. When students are asked to write down their own ideas, they are implementing the concept of being "Captain of their own ship." By explaining their ideas to others they are also exhibiting autonomy; the act of explaining one's ideas to others also represents a certain degree of a real-world skill. When the sharing activities are used to create a real-world product, the TV Reality show principle is applied. Students are applying the kaleidoscope principle by comparing and contrasting their thoughts with the thoughts and ideas of their partner. The "Rattle their cage" principle comes into play, not only when students are confronted with ideas from their partners that they may not fully understand or agree with, but also when they are expected to write these out.

A Further Look at Cooperative Learning

Cooperative learning provides an environment in which students can assist one another with tasks until the task is internalized. It provides the stimulus for restarting the cycle by giving each individual the opportunity to present knowledge the other has not internalized. The Association of American Colleges and Universities, through its initiative *Liberal Education and America's Promise (LEAP)*, had Peter D. Hart Research Associates (2006) conduct a survey of employers and recent college graduates. Their report examined the outcomes in college students that will make America competitive in the global economy. The results of the report indicate that both employers and recent graduates want to see more of an emphasis on skills that include teamwork skills, collaboration, and oral and written communication.

The research on cooperative learning has consistently shown its effectiveness. A meta-analysis conducted by Johnson et al. (1981) show that cooperation in a learning environment is more effective than interpersonal competition and individualistic efforts. A meta-analysis conducted by Zhining, Johnson, and Johnson (1995) demonstrated that "cooperative efforts produce higher-quality problem solving than do competitive efforts on a wide variety of problems that require different cognitive processes to solve" (p. 5).

Bowen (2000) conducted a study reporting on the effects of cooperative learning on chemistry achievement at the high-school and collegiate level. He reported on previous studies examining the effects of cooperative learning; the results from this meta-analysis indicate that cooperative learning has a positive effect on both academic achievement and attitude.

Marzano, Pickering, and Pollock (2001) examined some of the studies that attempted to synthesize the research on cooperative learning. This examination includes the Johnson et al. study previously cited in this section and other studies. They noted that all of these studies indicated that cooperative learning had a positive effect on students.

The research also has shown cooperative learning to be effective for a wide range of students from elementary students to the college-bound student. Wilson-Jones and Caston (2004) examined the effects of cooperative learning on African-American males in grades 3 through 6, and found that these students preferred to work in groups. Mesch, Johnson, and Johnson (1988) compared two groups of 10th-grade social studies students in a suburban setting. The group that was exposed to a cooperative team environment scored higher on tests about subject content. Significantly, although the study included four students with disabilities, the heterogeneous nature of the groups did not hamper the gains. Nichols and Miller (1994) examined how cooperative groups affected the motivation and achievement in Algebra II. The cooperative approach resulted in higher achievement than did the traditional approach of individual learning; moreover, the students in the cooperative environment were more motivated to learn. A subsequent study conducted by Nichols (1996) examined the effects of cooperative learning on geometry students. Students in the cooperative learning environment showed greater gains in geometry achievement and reported use of deeper processing strategies. Ghaith (2003) studied the relationship between cooperative, individualistic, and competitive forms of instruction in English as a foreign language and perceptions of the classroom climate. This study was conducted in a group of 135 university-bound students. The results indicated that not only was the cooperative learning treatment more effective, there was also a statistical significance between low and high group cooperation; the achievement level in the high cooperation group was higher. Doymus (2007) studied the effects of cooperative learning on 108 university students taking general chemistry. The students were split into two groups. One group was taught by traditional methods, the other through cooperative learning. The results from this study indicated that the group that was exposed to cooperative learning scored higher than the group that received traditional instruction.

5.2   Examples of Cooperative Learning Activities

What follows are exercises incorporating cooperative learning. To ensure that these activities follow Constructivist principles, as you read and connect these to your philosophy of teaching and learning, be sure to ask yourself the following questions:

- Are the students given autonomy to create their own version of knowledge?
- Are students learning through the process of teaching others and explaining to others?
- Are students expected to produce products in different modes?

- Are students classifying, predicting, and modifying knowledge, rather than just regurgitating knowledge?
- Are students required to think differently?
- Do students work with others, thus giving them the opportunity to interact with potential sources of contradiction?
- Are students presenting their learning in a format that is used in society? (Explaining information verbally and by the written word?)

EXERCISE 5.1:
Think/Write/Timed Pair Share

The teacher gets students into pairs as shown.

A B

Figure 5.2

The teacher gives a prompt, such as "What are the two most important things you learned in this class the last two weeks?" On the teacher's command, A shares with B for thirty seconds. On the teacher's command B shares with A. for thirty seconds. The teacher ensures that students are accountable for this activity. The teacher can do this by coordinating a class discussion on what students learned from their partner.

Notes: It is very important that the teacher keep accurate time. Also, this exercise enables students to become better listeners.

Adapted with permission from Kagan Publishing. Kagan, S. *Cooperative learning.* San Clemente, CA: Kagan Publishing,1994. www.KaganOnline.com

EXERCISE 5.2:
The Three-Step Interview

The teacher will get students into groups of four (see Figure 5.3).

A   B

C   D

Figure 5.3

Start with a Think/Share/Pair as before. After the Think/Share/Pair A and shares with C, and B shares with D. See Figure 5.4.

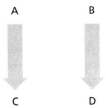

Figure 5.4

The group engages in a round robin, sharing their ideas. Students write a reflection on what they learned.

An extension of this activity, "the Toll Booth Problem," can be used at the end of class. Each student takes out a ½ sheet of paper. The teacher tells the students that this class will be treated as if it were the toll way; while traveling the toll way people must stop and pay a toll. So, in this class students, before they leave, must write on the piece of paper what they learned from any of their partners during the three-step interview.

Adapted with permission from Kagan Publishing. Kagan, S. *Cooperative learning.* San Clemente, CA: Kagan Publishing, 1994. www.KaganOnline.com

EXERCISE 5.3:

The Inside/Out Circle

The students are put in groups of two. The groups of two are then put into the positions as illustrated in the diagram. While the figure shows three groups, the number of groups is up to the teacher.

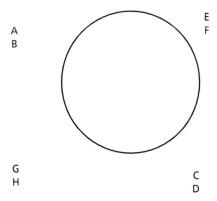

Figure 5.5

The teacher gives a prompt (as in the previous two examples). A shares with B, C shares with D, and E shares with F. Then they switch. On the signal from the teacher, the outer circle rotates in the direction chosen by the teacher. The new groups now share out before.

Notes: In a science lab the participants can stand at the corners of the lab table. A teacher can also use the perimeter of the entire room, and can have spots marked off on the floor. Then the teacher can have students rotate one spot, two spots, etc.

Adapted with permission from Kagan Publishing. Kagan, S. *Cooperative learning.* San Clemente, CA: Kagan Publishing, 1994. www.KaganOnline.com

EXERCISE 5.4:
Around the World

Before the class enters the room, the teacher puts chart paper in strategic places on the walls (each corner, in the middle of each wall, etc.).

On each piece of chart paper the teacher writes down a topic that the class has studied. For example, look at a math class. One topic could be combining like terms; another topic could be using the distributive law, etc.

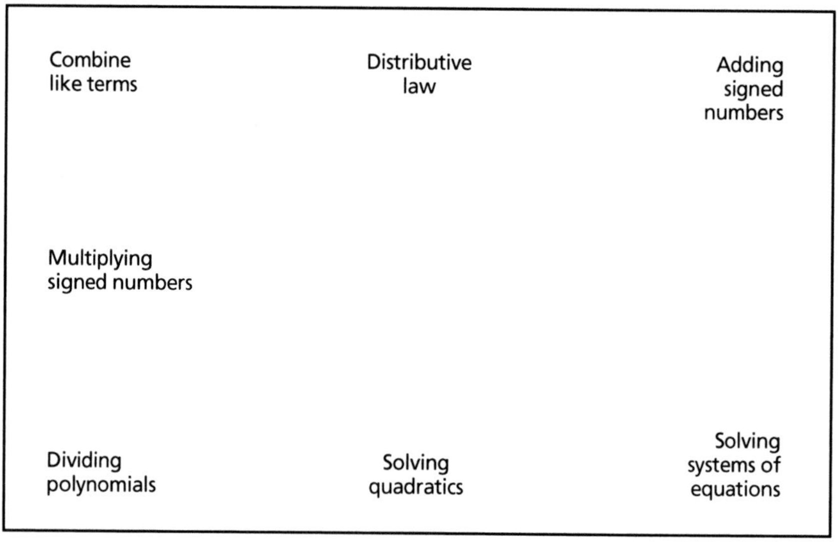

Combine like terms	Distributive law	Adding signed numbers
Multiplying signed numbers		
Dividing polynomials	Solving quadratics	Solving systems of equations

Figure 5.6

When students enter, they are put in groups. Each group starts at a chart and in the allotted time writes down as many ideas about that topic as it can come up with. On a signal from the teacher, each group rotates to the next sheet of paper. Depending on time, this rotating continues. After the last rotation, have the group categorize the lists.

Adapted from Saphier and Haley (1993a) *Activators: Activity Structures to Engage Students' Thinking Before Instruction,* published by Research for Better Teaching- www.RBTeach.com (The name of the activity has also been changed.)

EXERCISE 5.5:
3–2–1

This exercise is usually used as a summary activity. It can be done individually or as part of a group. The generic form is as follows:

- ▪ Write 3 things that you really liked.
- ▪ Write 2 things that you would like to know more about.
- ▪ Write 1 thing that is an example of the concept.

A specific form for a history class is the following:

- ▪ Write 3 strengths of a leader during the period you are studying.
- ▪ Identify 2 important people in that person's life. Briefly mention the importance.
- ▪ Describe 1 weakness in that person.

Or, for a math class, studying a new math definition:

- ▪ Give 3 examples of an integer.
- ▪ Give 2 examples of a number that is not an integer.
- ▪ Add 1 sentence or clause that qualifies the definition to exclude one of your specific examples.

Notes: Variations come from the writing prompts. One variation is to have students give a nonexample. Another prompt that can be used is to have students discuss two activities that helped them learn.

Adapted from Saphier and Haley (1993b) *Summarizers: Activity Structures to Support Integration and Retention of New Learning,* published by Research for Better Teaching- www.RBTeach.com.

EXERCISE 5.6:
I Spy

The teacher begins with an activity in which students are in a group. On a signal given by the teacher, one student from a two-student group rotates to another group ("the spy"). The "spy" takes notes on what the other group does. The "spy" returns and briefs the partner.

Then roles are reversed, and the other student becomes the spy and rotates to a group different from the first rotation.

Notes: It is important that each partner assumes accountability by becoming the "spy."

To increase the autonomy and the possibility of creating a product or "mental space," a writing prompt can be used. Prompts, such as "What surprised you," "What would you not use," and "Are you seeing any trends, and please explain why," will empower students to create new connections ("Turn the kaleidoscope").

Adapted with permission from Kagan Publishing. Kagan, S. *Cooperative learning*. San Clemente, CA: Kagan Publishing, 1994. www.KaganOnline.com

---

5.3   Cooperative Learning and Constructivism

Now that you have gone over some cooperative learning activities, it is important to formally analyze these to ensure that they follow Constructivist principles. To this end, let us consider the following questions:

A. **Are the students given autonomy to create their own version of knowledge?**

   When students are enabled to think about what they learned, rank what are the most important elements in their group, develop questions and construct answers to these questions, modify the thoughts of their fellow students, and modify their own learning by blending the ideas of others with thoughts of others, students are engaged in the process of creating their own knowledge. The two-box induction activity enables students to create two versions of the definitions.

B. **Are students learning through the process of teaching others, and explaining to others?**

   Activities such as Think/Write/Time Pair Share, and Three Step Interview, and empower students to do this by their very nature.

C. **Are students expected to produce products in different modes?**

   A graphics organizer can be used with many cooperative learning exercises. Also, writing assignments such as short summaries can be added.

D. **Are students classifying, predicting, modifying knowledge, rather than just regurgitating knowledge?**

While all cooperative learning activities have these activities embedded in them, Exercises 5.5 and 5.6 are structured precisely by these cognitive activities.

E. Are students required to think differently?

All cooperative learning activities, if properly managed, can do this. Many cooperative learning activities can use prompts such as "How did you change?", "What exactly was done in class today that enabled you to change?", or "What did you do today that helped another student to change their way of thinking?"

F. Do students work with others, thus giving them the opportunity to interact with potential sources of contradiction?

The effective use of some of the strategies for forming groups will provide opportunities for working with different people.

G. Are students presenting their learning in a format that is used in society (explaining information verbally and by the written word)?

These are all major components of the cooperative learning activities that are presented in this chapter.

Through cooperative learning, the teacher can create a Constructivist learning environment. In such an environment students work with others to create and modify their own knowledge base by presenting their knowledge in different formats, blending the knowledge of others with their own knowledge, and working with others to create solutions to problems and to create predictions and hypotheses.

6

The Linguistic Mode and Questioning

While cooperative learning creates an environment in which the student creates knowledge through interaction with other students, it is important to examine how the teacher, especially through questioning, can create a Constructivist environment. This chapter looks at the role of questioning in establishing a Constructivist environment.

6.1 Questioning Techniques

On the topic of questioning, Marzano, Pickering, and Pollock (2001) stated that "questioning might account for as much as 80 percent of what occurs in a given classroom" (p. 113). The bad news is that "most of the questions teachers ask are lower order in nature" (p. 113). Thus, higher-level thinking such as explaining, categorizing, predicting, and hypothesizing, which is Constructivist in nature, are not frequently seen in many classrooms. This bad news was earlier seen by Gall (1984), who noted that although teachers recognize "the effectiveness of higher cognitive questions, most teachers do not emphasize them in practice" (p. 42).

The Comprehensive Handbook of Constructivist Teaching, pages 63–76
Copyright © 2010 by Information Age Publishing
All rights of reproduction in any form reserved.

Renaud and Murray (2007) found that gains in the critical thinking of students can be predicted by the frequency of the higher-order questions that are asked; Renaud and Murray examined three other studies. One study compared the number of higher-order questions in assignments and tests in actual classes to pre-/post-test gains in critical thinking. The second study compared two groups of students given lower- versus higher-level questions in actual studies. The third study was a true laboratory study relating level of review questions to pretest and posttest gains. Renaud and Murray, in examining all three studies, found that students increase their critical thinking skills when they experience higher-order questions.

Redfield and Rousseau (1981) used a meta-analytic technique to study the relationship between the level of teacher questioning and student achievement. They analyzed twenty studies on teacher use of higher and lower level questions. Their examination indicated that gains in student achievement can be expected when higher cognitive questions take on a prominent role during classroom instruction.

The concept of *elaborative interrogation*, a technique that enables learners to connect their prior knowledge with an upcoming topic, was investigated by Woloshyn et al. (1990). This technique involves having students answer "why questions" about facts or readings (Why does this fact make sense to you, given what you know about _____ ? With what you know, why did the lead character in the play do that? Why would the main character choose _____ instead of _____ ?).Clearly, this technique has Constructivist characteristics. The student does not replicate an isolated fact but must work on his knowledge and connect it to other pieces of knowledge. The researchers found that this technique helped adults learn facts that were presented in paragraph form. An important observation from this study was that it did not matter whether the answer was adequate. Rather, the very attempt to generate the correct answer was the important parameter. Wood, Pressley, and Winne (1990) studied the effects of elaborative interrogation on children's learning of factual content. As with the adult study, the researchers found definite gains even when the generated question was not correct. Ozgungor and Guthrie (2004) reported that college students who attempted to answer elaborative interrogation questions embedded within the text they were required to read recalled more information, had more effective coherent mental representations, and recognized more correct inferences. Elaborative interrogation, by combining prior knowledge with the process of explaining answers, is a proven Constructivist technique.

6.2 The Knowledge Level of Bloom's Taxonomy and Constructivism

One instrument for analyzing the cognitive level of questioning techniques is Bloom's taxonomy, which is a hierarchy that classifies thinking patterns. We look at Bloom's taxonomy as a means for creating a Constructivist environment, but before this we need to look at some items concerning questioning in classrooms. Following is a summary of this taxonomy and how it can be used to create a Constructivist environment.

6.2.1 The Knowledge Level of Bloom's Taxonomy and Constructivism

The knowledge level is categorized by recalling information or data. An example would be a person quoting prices to a customer. Another example would be a student reciting the Gettysburg address, or an engineer recalling what the sine ratio in trigonometry is. Words or phrases describing this level are

- List;
- Match;
- Recall;
- Recognize;
- State;
- Know;
- Name;
- Which is true or false?;
- Which answer is correct?

The activities at this level provide little opportunity for the student to show autonomy, make connections with other knowledge bases, explain to others, or modify what they already know. It does not involve the processes of the student putting knowledge in a different form, connecting previously disconnected information to form a new whole, or using previously learned information to solve a real-world, messy problem.

6.2.2 The Comprehension Level of Bloom's Taxonomy and Constructivism

The comprehension level is the level in which a person explains, estimates, gives examples, restates, and paraphrases.

The following words describing this level:

- Classify;
- Cite;

- Describe;
- Explain;
- Give examples;
- Illustrate;
- Restate;
- Reword;
- Summarize.

While not all of these activities at this level will be Constructivist, this level does provide some possibilities for creating a Constructivist environment. Classification involves the process of creating a category, and rewording involves the creation of meaning by connecting a known concept to different words. Giving an example means that the students are connecting their version of a category to something they already know. Rewording involves the process of creating new words and phrases to express an already existing idea or concept. These cognitive activities are Constructive in nature because they involve student autonomy in explaining to others. Moreover, they enable students to make connections to knowledge bases that were previously unconnected.

Examples of a Constructivist question at this level follow:

- I like what you said—will you rephrase it so we can make sure that the entire class hears it?
- Sue, will you give an example of what you just said?
- Bill, you just heard what Sue said; will you tell us in your own words what she said?
- Jane, you gave me some nice examples; can you give me some nonexamples?
- Tammera and Joyce just presented some very interesting ideas. In a few seconds I will call on someone to use his own words to summarize what they said.

These examples illustrate that the student is just not supplying or reciting an isolated fact or repeating a previous fact; the student must connect this knowledge to other pieces of knowledge and create new words to describe this knowledge. These examples illustrate the autonomy of the student.

6.2.3   The Application Level of Bloom's Taxonomy and Constructivism

The application level is one in which the student uses previously learned concepts and facts in a new situation in order to solve a new problem. The following key words and phrases that describe this level are

- Solve by using this theorem;
- Give me an example;
- Classify;
- Use.

Questions from this level that represent the Constructivist philosophy follow:

1. In a business class: the teacher asks, "How can we use the marketing strategy we just learned to market a new product?"
2. In a geometry class, the teacher says, "What is an example of what we have just discussed?"
3. In a history class, the teacher asks, "Could this have happened ten years later? Why/Why not?"
4. In a social studies class the teacher asks, "What questions would you ask of Martin Luther King Jr. that follow from our discussion?"
5. In an English class the teacher asks, "How does what happened to the character in the story relate to something in your own life?"

Student autonomy is evident in these examples; the student is connecting to personal experiences and beliefs, creating personal examples of concepts, and hypothesizing.

6.2.4 The Analysis Level of Bloom's Taxonomy and Constructivism

At the analysis level students rework their prior knowledge by putting it into categories that they create. This reworking of knowledge is also characterized by distinguishing between facts and inferences. Key words for this level follow:

- Compare;
- Contrast;
- Analyze;
- Examine;
- Distinguish;
- Separate;
- Explain.

Examples of using the analytic level to create a Constructivist environment follow:

1. How is this different from . . . ?
2. What are the commonalities between the two readings?

3. In an Algebra II class the teacher says "Let compare Dan's method of using the quadratic formula to solve the problem with Barb's method of completing the square."

4. In a literature class, after the students have read "I hear America Singing," the teacher says, "What is the theme of this piece?" Later, the teacher says, "How does this compare with President Obama's ideas?"

The students, in these cases, are acting with autonomy by creating categories to put their ideas into and to compare and contrast ideas. These processes represent the Constructivist activity of making connections.

6.2.5 The Synthesis Level of Bloom's Taxonomy and Constructivism

At this level the student is fully engaged in Constructivist activities by creating, planning for, and designing products, inventing procedures, making predictions, hypothesizing, and proposing other procedures. The following key words describe these activities:

- Create;
- Invent;
- Formulate;
- Predict;
- Compose;
- Plan;
- Predict;
- Hypothesize.

Some examples follow:

1. Write your feelings about some of the new techniques demonstrated in class.

2. Create a rap song that summarizes what we did in class?

3. In a home economics class, the teacher says, "Using the ideas we have discussed in class, create a new recipe."

4. In a history class, the teacher would ask, "If Harry Truman was President during the 1960s instead of LBJ, how would he have handled the Vietnam situation?"

5. In a biology class, the teacher asks, "How would Darwin look at the animal rights groups in the world today?"

6.2.6 The Evaluation Level of Bloom's Taxonomy and Constructivism

The evaluation level of Bloom's taxonomy provides the teacher the opportunity to create a thoroughly Constructivist environment. Here the student constructs judgments and appraisals about the value of the ideas of other students. Key words characterizing this level are as follows:

- Judge;
- Justify;
- Verify;
- Decide which method is your preference and discuss this;
- Choose the best method and discuss;
- Recommend.

Examples of using the evaluation level to create a Constructivist environment follow:

1. In a math class, the teacher says, "Determine if Tom's method for doing problem six is more effective than the method presented by the book."
2. In a literature class, the teacher says, "Would the poem been more effective if it was written in a different rhyme scheme? Be prepared to discuss your reasoning."
3. In a literature class, the teacher says, "Robert Frost once said that a poem 'begins as a lump in the throat, a sense of wrong, homesickness, and loneliness.' Do you think that this description applies to the poem we have just studied? Be prepared to justify your reasoning."
4. In a history class, a teacher says, "John Kennedy said 'Don't ask what your country can do for you, but ask what you can do for your country.' Do you think that this would be an effective theme for a presidential campaign? Be prepared to defend your position."

These prompts represent the Constructivist activities of autonomy, making connections (Turn the kaleidoscope) and creating new ways of thinking (Rattle their cage). The prompts presented empower students to "work on knowledge," not just reciting what the teacher said or what they already know. By participating in the above prompts students must explain their ideas orally and in written words, connect their understanding to new experiences, create judgments, and construct the words to justify those judgments.

6.3 Other Taxonomies

While Bloom's taxonomy provides a well-known template for the Constructivist teacher, other formats and frameworks contain similar Constructivist guidelines presented by Bloom. For example, Marzano (1993) presented a simplified system; his template is a two-part taxonomy, composed of recitation questions and construction questions.

A more elaborate scheme, presented by Walsh and Sattes (2005), involves a system developed by Gallagher and Aschner. This taxonomy consists of three levels: recall, convergent, and divergent. In this scheme, recall questions are not of the Constructivist level; convergent questions ask for the student to supply one correct answer, while divergent questions enable the student to take different paths in order to answer. Divergent questions provide the potential for the student to engage in autonomy, turn the kaleidoscope, and have their cage rattled, and they are also the questions need to solve authentic situations.

A second system presented by Walsh and Satte consists of three levels: recall, use, and create. The "use" and "create" levels provide a Constructivist environment. Still another framework they presented is that of "questioning circles," first introduced by Christenbury and Kelly (1983). Imagine three intersecting circles, with the first representing subject area, the second representing personal knowledge, and the third circle representing other subjects. It is the intersection of the three circles (intersecting domains) that is of interest to the Constructivist teacher.

Here are examples of the use of such questioning circles.

1. **Individual Domain Questions**:
   - The Subject: Define what authentic assessment is.
   - Personal Knowledge: Have you ever been exposed to authentic assessment during your time here at the university?
   - Other Subjects: On your job or in extracurricular activities, what type of assessment was used?
2. **Overlap Questions**:
   Subject/Personal Domains
   - If you were a teacher, what type of authentic assessment would you use? Be prepared to defend your answer.

   Subject/Personal/Other Domains
   - Consider the situation where your principal calls you into the office and wants you to stop using authentic assessment in

your daily teaching. Create a response defending your use of authentic assessment. Your defense must include a reference to skills employers say are needed in the 21st century and motivational theories.

In Chapter 14, we will provide details on another possible framework for forming Constructivist questions, based on metacognition. Briefly, metacognition is the process of thinking about one's thinking. While Chapter 14 will examine the importance by presenting research and possible prompts, here are a few prompts that will get you going.

- What step of the proof still confuses you?
- What surprised you in today's lesson?
- What class activity enabled you to think differently?

Another framework that could be used either independently or with other frameworks is the Standard Six that is presented in this book. Whatever taxonomy is used, it is important that the Constructivist teacher monitor how classroom question creates and maintains a Constructivist environment.

6.4 Expanded Activities Using Constructivist Questioning Techniques

This section presents expanded activities of using Constructivist questioning techniques.

EXERCISE 6.1:
Using Constructivist Questioning in a Literature Class

The students read Robert Frost's poem, *The Road Not Taken*, reproduced below.

Two roads diverged in a yellow wood,
And sorry I could not travel both.
And be one traveler, long I stood
And looked down one as far as I could

Then took the other, as just as fair,
And having perhaps the better claim,
Because it was grassy and wanted wear;
Though as for that, the passing there
Had worn them really about the same,

And both that morning equally lay
In leaves no step had trodden black.
Oh, I kept the first for another day!
Yet knowing how way leads on to way,
I doubted if I should ever come back.

I shall be telling this with a sigh
Somewhere ages and ages hence:
Two roads diverged in a wood, and I-
I took the one less traveled by,
And that has made all the difference.

The teacher creates a Constructivist environment by asking the following questions:

- Look at the first paragraph. Can you summarize it in your own words? (Comprehension)
- If the speaker in this poem were alive, how would he describe his philosophy of life? (Analysis and Application)
- What types of life decisions is the speaker referring to? Be prepared to discuss and defend your point. (Synthesis)
- Robert Frost once said that a poem "begins as a lump in the throat, a sense of wrong, homesickness, a loneliness." Do you think that this description applies to the poem we have just studied? Be prepared to justify your reasoning. (Evaluation)
- Would recommend to your best friend to take the "road less traveled?" (Evaluation)

EXERCISE 6.2:
Using Constructivist Questioning in a History Class

The teacher is about to begin to discuss the current conflict in Iraq. She plans to start this out by discussing the concept of "winning a war." She starts out by saying, "Take an example from the history of World War II. While on the surface it appears as if the Allies won the war, the historian Richard Overy reminds us otherwise." She then has the class read the following excerpt from Overy's book:

When people heard that the title of my next book was to be "Why the Allies Won," it often provoked the retort: "Did they?" There are many ways of winning. With the passage of time it has become possible to argue that none of the three major Allies—Britain, the United States and the Soviet Union—won a great deal. Britain lost her empire and her leading world role; the United States that they traded one European enemy for another. (p. xiii)

The teacher then encourages a discussion by using the following questions:

- How can we use Overy's ideas to create a definition of "winning a war" (Application, Synthesis)
- Overy implies that the Axis powers won the war. Do you agree? Be prepared to defend your response. (Application, Synthesis, Evaluation)
- Using your own definition of winning a war, do you think that the US won the Vietnam War? Using Overy's definition, do you think the US won? How does your definition differ from Overy's? How does this difference influence how the question is answered? (Analysis, Application, Synthesis, Evaluation).

Note: These questions enable the student to act autonomously, experience ideas different from their own, and make connections to these ideas.

EXERCISE 6.3:
Using Constructivist Questioning and Film Clips—A Collegiate Assessment Class

This example is from an education class at the collegiate level. The class is studying authentic assessment.

The teacher starts out by showing a film clip from the movie Top Gun. In the scene shown the students are sitting in an auditorium watching videos of themselves in a dogfight. The instructors are critiquing student performance and discussing their remarks with the students.

The teacher asks the following questions:

- We are all familiar with paper and pencil assessments. Does this scene, while not of that format, still represent assessment? Be prepared to defend your answer. (Analysis, Synthesis)
- In this type of assessment, what is the role of the teacher? Of the student? Are these roles different from the roles of traditional paper and pencil assessment? (Analysis, Synthesis)
- In your opinion, are today's students ready to take on the roles required of them in authentic assessment? If not, what will you do as a teacher, to ensure that they are ready?
- This type of assessment is called authentic assessment. Based on this example, write down your definition of authentic assessment. (Application, Synthesis)

- John, how does your definition differ from Sue's? (Analysis)
- What are the advantages and disadvantages of authentic assessment? (Analysis, Synthesis)
- Think of the content area in which you want to teach. Write down an example of authentic assessment from that content area. (Application, Analysis)
- In your opinion, can authentic assessment be used as an instrument to prepare students for high-stakes testing? (Application, Synthesis, Evaluation)

This example illustrates a Constructivist classroom. By writing down and stating their own opinions and definitions of authentic assessment, the students are applying the principle of Be Captain of your own Ship. They are applying the TV reality show principle when they create an example of authentic assessment that they would use in their own practice. When they do this and compare their ideas with those of their classmates, they are applying the Kaleidoscope principle. By comparing authentic assessment to traditional assessment, including the roles of teachers and students, the "Rattle their Cage" principle comes into play.

EXERCISE 6.4:
Using Constructivist Questioning in Biology

The teacher poses the following questions to students in a class studying Darwin.

- Darwin a century ago argued that human facial expressions are universal. What is really being said here? (Analysis, Synthesis)
- Did Darwin mean that if we told people from 4 different countries that their child had died, they would have (almost) the same expression? (Application)
- Does that mean expressions are biologically determined, rather than culturally learned? (Application, Synthesis) If expressions are not culturally determined, what are the implications of this? (Application, Synthesis)
- How does Darwin's view connect to cloning? (Application)

6.5 Constructivism and Expanded Questioning Techniques

The preceding expanded questioning techniques provide more techniques for the teacher to create a Constructivist environment. These activities require the students, not to just repeat memorized facts, but rather to create their own thoughts by connecting previously unconnected learnings, predicting and hypothesizing, finding personal relevance, applying their knowledge to previously unaddressed situations, and comparing and contrasting different views.

Since the theories and examples of Constructivist questioning are intended to lead to class discussion, it is important to examine the nature of discussion in general.

Student discussion has long been considered valuable, but you might wonder whether research supports this premise. The answer is yes. For but one example, Applebee et al. (2003) examined 64 middle and secondary English classrooms in order to understand the relationship between discussion-based teaching and student literacy performance. Their results indicate that students whose classrooms emphasize discussion internalize the knowledge and skills necessary to engage in challenging literacy tasks on their own.

Kahn (2007) confirmed these results when she wrote, "It is engagement in authentic or dialogic discussion—as opposed to recitation—that results in enhanced literature achievement and reading comprehension" (p. 1). The distinction between recitation and discussion is critical. Dillon (1984) notes that "discussion calls for complex thinking processes and attitude change" (p. 51). He expands on this by stating that discussion involves "soliciting student opinions and thought, not just right answers" (p. 51).

Connecting to others' ideas and constructing and changing thoughts are all Constructivist actions, but how do we make this happen in the classroom? One answer is to introduce conflict or controversy (Kahn, 2007, p. 2). Now, how can we implement this strategy? One way would to use controversial prompts in the cooperative learning activities already described.

6.6 Creating a Constructivist Questioning Plan

Questioning, like all effective teaching methods, must be the result of an ongoing plan. The Constructivist teacher, in order to create an environment structured by the four characteristics, must carefully implement questioning. Figure 6.1 illustrates the questioning process that includes choosing a taxonomy, using the Standard Six, and also utilizing other Constructivist principles.

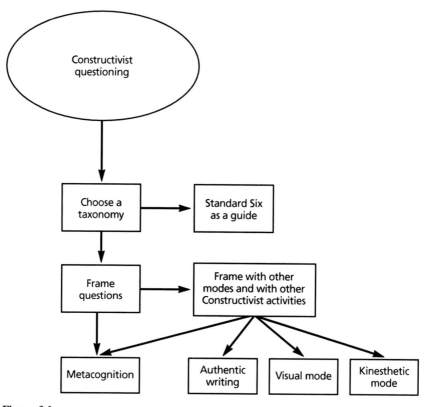

Figure 6.1

7

The Linguistic Mode and Authentic Writing

$\mathbf{A}$s we've noted several times, using real-world learning is an effective Constructivist precept. Duke et al. (2006/2007) reported that teachers who used authentic literacy activities in their teaching "had students who showed higher growth in both comprehension and writing" (p. 2). The Constructivist calls such activities authentic writing.

7.1 Writing in Context and Constructivism

Let's take a look at what has been said concerning authentic writing and the linguistic mode.

Knowledge is an entity that is situated in context. Brown, Collins, and Duguid (1989) pointed out that "people generally learn words in the context of ordinary communication" (p. 32). They expand on this concept by stating that "the average 17-year-old has learned vocabulary at a rate of 5,000 words per year (13 per day) for over 16 years" (p. 32). Comparing the

The Comprehensive Handbook of Constructivist Teaching, pages 77–88
Copyright © 2010 by Information Age Publishing
77

teaching of language in context to teaching language as an isolated activity, they wrote: "Teaching from dictionaries assumes that definitions and exemplary sentences are self-contained 'pieces' of knowledge. But words and sentences are not islands, entire unto themselves" (p. 32). The learning of language in context is then extended to learning in general: "All knowledge is, we believe, like language. Its constituent parts index the world and so are inextricably a product of the activity and situations in which they are produced" (p. 33).

The process of learning language does not occur in an isolated, abstract setting Duke et al. (2007), in examining the genre for developing comprehension and writing, studied authentic literacy and concluded that "students learn language not in abstract, decontextualized terms, but in application, in a context that language is really for" (p. 345).

Authentic writing also has its advocates at the collegiate level. Monroe (2003), in examining the difference between "writing across the curriculum and "writing in the disciplines," touched on the theme of having students create authentic literary products. Monroe wrote: "A first-year writing requirement embedded in the disciplines signals that all writing takes place in particular contexts, for particular purposes and audiences" (p. 5). The phrase "embedded in the disciplines reflects the Constructivist activity of connecting to a real-world situation.

The National Assessment of Educational Progress (NAEP), the only federal test in America, has also seen the importance of authentic writing (2008). Its writing assessment has the goals of narrative writing, informative writing, and persuasive writing. It defines narrative writing as the creation of stories or personal essays, and informative writing as writing that conveys messages, instructions, and ideas. Persuasive writing is defined as the writing of letters to friends, newspapers, and employers. The NAEP interpretation of authentic writing connects with the Constructivist concept of creating an authentic product.

Newell and Winograd (1989) studied the effects of different types of writing. In their study, which examined the writing of eight eleventh–grade students, these tasks consisted of note-taking, answering study questions, and essay writing.

Authentic writing, the type of writing that is done in every aspect of everyday life, is a Constructivist activity. Connecting content knowledge to a specific everyday context and to a particular form of written communication empowers writers to construct their own form of knowledge; this is Constructivism in every aspect.

7.2   Authentic Writing and Motivation

The foundations of our Constructivist practice include student autonomy and real-life products, and authentic writing provides a platform for implementing these constructs. Bruning and Horn (2000) viewed writing in the typical classroom as "not set within larger social or communication frames that can create interest and a sense of writing's relevance" (p. 30). They believe that authentic tasks empower students to "develop one or more distinctive styles of writing" (p. 30), and also empower students to create more complex versions of voice, such as writing with irony or with authority.

In addressing student autonomy and empowerment, Oldfather (1993) stressed that students need to choose personally relevant projects and writing topics, and that "their voices have been heard" (p. 680). A Constructivist version of authentic writing can provide guidelines in this direction.

Writing in authentic contexts can provide Constructivist teachers with the environment for empowering students to become self-motivated to create products that are embedded with curricular goals and objectives. The next section presents guidelines for authentic writing in the Constructivist classroom.

7.3   The Constructivist Model for Authentic Writing

The model that follows will be an effective tool for the Constructivist teacher.

The Constructivist Model for Authentic Writing

1. Involve the creation of a product.
2. Have a specific purpose
3. Involve the use of a type of writing style that is used or seen in everyday life.
4. Allow for some student choice.
5. Be accompanied by a reflection that empowers students to think about how the assignment helped them learn the content, and helped them in general. Below is a suggested template:
   a. What did you know about (the content) before this writing assignment?
   b. During this writing assignment, what did you learn that surprised you?
   c. What part of the writing assignment helped you learn about (the content) that another assignment might not have been able to do?

    d. After comparing your assignment with those of others, what would you incorporate or use from others? How would these ideas help you understand the (content)? How would these ideas help you learn about the writing type-poem, newspaper article, etc.

7.4   Constructivism and Authentic Products

The remainder of the chapter is devoted to exercises and actual student results. These examples include a magazine article, a newspaper article, and a letter to the governor. The Constructivist theme of embedding content within each authentic product is seen in each exercise.

EXERCISE 7.1:
Writing a Manual

This exercise is a takeoff of the "X for Dummies" series of books. Instead of doing the traditional method of review for a test, students are asked to design their own manual based on the topic to be tested.

    To make this activity more "authentic," the teacher should allow the students to use this manual on the test. The following are actual pages from two student-created manuals, "Factoring for Dummies."

    Notes: One variation that will provide interesting results is that of not telling the students immediately that they can use the manual on the test. After students have settled in and are actively engaged in this activity, tell them that they can use the manual.

    The teacher can keep track of how many students really do *not* use the manual during the test. It may be because the writing of the manual empowered them to create a strong network of ideas.

Figure 7.1

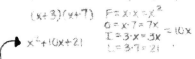

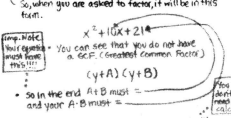

Figure 7.2

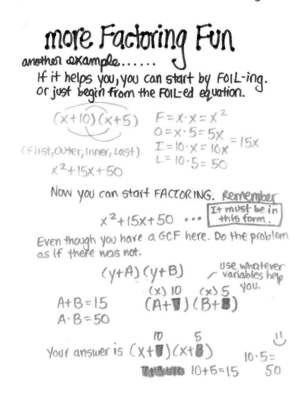

Figure 7.3

EXERCISE 7.2:

Writing a Gaming Proposal

In this assignment students are playing the role of a creative director for a gaming company. They are to design a game "of chance" and write a proposal for this game to a prospective buyer, Mr. M. T. Pockets. Figures 7.4, 7.5, and 7.6 show an example of student work for this assignment. A second example of student work is shown by Figures 7.7 and 7.8.

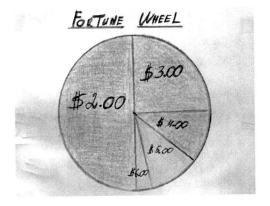

Figure 7.4

May 10, 2003

M.T. Pockets
526 E. Madison Dr.
Las Vegas NV. 50652

Dear Mr. Pockets,

I was very pleased to work for you and help you to design a new game that does not involve any specific skills. The game, as you requested, is totally based on randomness.

What I did, was I designed a game, like roulette. I named it **"Fortune Wheel"**. The game board is colored with a five different colors, and is marked with an actual amount of money that you can win.

The mechanics of the game is very simple. The payer has to spin, and on what amount of money did the arrow stopped, it would be an amount that player would win.

As you can see, this game is very simple and wouldn't cost you a lot of money actually to invent this game and start to play.

Also, to make things easier for you, I did some calculations on your expected profit, if you would choose to play my game.

Suppose that it cost $3.50 to play this game.

There is 50% of chance to win $2.00.
25% of chance to win $3.00
10% of chance to win $4.00
10% of chance to win $5.00
And only 5% of chance to win $6.00.

So....

$(.50)(-2.00) + (.25)(-3.00) + (.1)(-4.00) + (.1)(-5.00) + (.05)(-6.00) = -1 + -.75 + -.4 + -.5 + -.3 = \$-2.95.$

So it would give you:

$3.50 - $2.95 = \$ .55 per spin (that money would go right into your pocket).

Figure 7.5

I also looked into the possibility, where, what if $4.00 payoff was raised to $4.50. What would be the average expected payoff?

That would give you:

(.50)(-2.00) + (.25)(-3.00) + (.1)(-4.50) + (.1)(5.00) + (.05)(-6.00) = -1 + -.75 + -.45 + .5 + -.3 = $ -3.00

So it would give you:

$ 3.50 - $ 3.00 = $ .50 per spin. (This money would go right into your pocket).

As you can see, you would make a lot of money by inventing this game. It would be a popular game because it wouldn't cot a lot of money for the people to play this game, an it doesn't requires any skills to play it.

My suggestions would be, that you would stick with this plan of game, because it will make fortunes, as far as right now, this is what you're looking for.

Sincerely

Figure 7.6

Big Time Gaming
12345 S. Sunset Blvd.
Las Vegas, Nevada
66689

M.T. Pockets
Big Time Gaming CEO
12345 S. Sunset Blvd.
Las Vegas, Nevada
66689

Dear Mr. M.T. Pockets,

Here at *Big Time Gaming*, we are concerned with making quality games that will attract a crowd. Well my associate and I have come up with a game called "Spin-a-Chance". This game can be played and understood by virtually all patrons. The more patrons playing our game, the more profit to be earned. So here is how the game works...the spinner is divided into 4 parts. Each part has a number value (i.e.: 1=$1.00, 2=$2.00, 3=$3.00, and 4=$4.00). The patron pays $3.00 to play the game. They spin the spinner once, and whatever number they land on is the amount paid out to the patron. Since we divided the spinner into four sections, its like a pie. Each section is worth a different decimal amount. The largest section is .5 or $\frac{1}{2}$. The second section is $\frac{1}{4}$ or .25. The other two sections are 1/8 or .125 each. The probability equation is:

5(-1)+ 25(-2)+ 125(-3)+ 125(-4)

Figure 7.7

Probability is your chances of winning the game, and the total
number of positive outcomes. On average, we pay $1.88 to each
player per spin. Our profit for Spin-a-Chance is amount paid per
game minus average amount paid per player. This equals $1.12. I
hope you find our information to be useful in your consideration
of our game. If you have any questions, please fill free to contact
us. Thanks again!

Sincerely,

Figure 7.8

EXERCISE 7.3:
Writing a Letter to the Governor

In this math example, students are working as an advisor to the governor of
Idaho. The governor is concerned that the annual increase in registered vehicles will result in the state running out of numbers for the license plates.
The students are told that the governor is expecting an increase of 8%
annually. In this exercise the students apply their knowledge of compound
interest to the increase of license plates; they then use their knowledge of
permutations and combinations to construct a system for arranging letters
and numbers on the license plates. The students are required to write a letter to the governor explaining their system.

   Notes: Teacher may want to use their state's numbers in this problem,
and may want to contact their state concerning some data on the number
of registered vehicles, what the state does not like about their current sys-

tem of license plates, etc. A similar problem could be set up regarding the number of phone numbers available.

Following is a student response to the assignment.

Dear Governor and State Legislature,

My partner and I did the research to find out how many license plates will be needed in ten years. We also did the research to find out what would be the cheapest arrangement of letters and numbers. We came to the conclusion that there will be 1,602,880 license plates needed in the next ten years. To get this toe took the number of 784,135 license plates that the state currently has and multiplied it by the rate of 8% which represents how much the number of registered vehicles will increase. We raised the rate to the tenth power to represent the 10 years. Four symbol license plates will not work because you will only have enough combinations for 67,600 plates. The best way to do the license plates is to with two numbers and three letters. By doing so, you will have enough plates for 1,757,600 plates. The advantage of this combination is that you will have enough combinations for the state. It is also the cheapest combination possible for the next ten years. The disadvantage is that it's not perfect so it will leave you with more plates than you will need. We hope that you appreciate our help and use it wisely. We enjoyed helping you.

Figure 7.9

EXERCISE 7.4:

Writing a newsletter to parents explaining what a standard score is and what it means.

This is can be used in a Tests and Measurements class. Students are given the following scenario.

You are talking with some colleagues right after your first Parent Teachers Night. The principal joins the conversation. You share one conversation in which one parent stated that his daughter scored a 26 on the ACT, but he really doesn't understand what this means, nor is he sure what the ACT is really about. He adds that the report talks about this "benchmark stuff" but admits that he is confused. Two of your fellow teachers relate similar stories. The next day the principal contacts you and states that he has heard many of the same stories from other teachers. He wants you to head a project that will educate parents on the meaning of these standardized test scores. He has indicated to you that you must either design a web site or write a short manual or design a newsletter explaining what a standard score means.

You must create a newsletter, or a manual, or a web page that does the following:

- Explain what the philosophy/purpose of the ACT is.
- Explain what the ACT measures.
- Explain to a parent what the ACT scores means and also explain the meaning of the benchmarks.
- Explain to parents at a level that they will understand. Remember, many parents do not study math every day.
- Explain what the normal curve is (in terms of a distribution).
- Explain what a standard score is, how it relates to the normal curve, how it relates to a percentile.
- Give at least two examples of how to use a standard score to determine a percentile for a student for the ACT.
- Explain what the benchmarks explain.

You are to write a one-page reflection on this assignment. You may use one or all of the following prompts (if you wish to use your own prompts, please see the instructor).

EXERCISE 7.5:

Writing a newspaper article about the Mexican War—An example from American history

At the time of the Mexican War, public opinion was divided. Some people, like Abraham Lincoln, opposed the war. Also, at the time California was a part of Mexico. This background information leads to the requirements of this assignment. Students are asked to write a newspaper article describing the outbreak of the Mexican War. Some are to write the article for a newspaper owned by a Mexican person living in California. Other students write the article for a newspaper owned by Americans living in California. A third group of students write for a newspaper located in Illinois that supports the war. A fourth group of students can write the article for a newspaper owned by a friend of President Polk.

Notes: It is important that students refer to the historic facts in this assignment. It is also important to find examples of newspaper writing from that era to show to students.

8

Creating a Constructivist Environment through Visual Literacy

Let's do a quick exercise to get ourselves thinking about the visual mode. Take out a piece of paper and a pencil. Draw the first thing that comes to your mind when I say "hot dog." Now look on the following image, and compare your drawing with what I had in mind.

Figure 8.1

Burmark, L. (2002). *Visual literacy: Learn to see. See to learn.* Alexandria, VA: Association for Supervision and Curriculum Development.

The Comprehensive Handbook of Constructivist Teaching, pages 89–107
Copyright © 2010 by Information Age Publishing

I bet that you were not thinking in this direction, but that is the point: the visual mode is powerful and, as this example demonstrates, has the ability to be precise. Visual literacy, as demonstrated by our exercise, is an important intellectual skill that we would all like our students to develop. As Constructivist teachers, you can use strategies to capitalize on the visual mode in your practice.

In this chapter we examine visual literacy, or the visual mode, by focusing on three questions:

1. What is visual literacy—or what does the visual mode consist of?
2. Why is the visual mode so important?
3. How can we as Constructivist educators use the visual mode or visual literacy to create a Constructivist environment?

8.1 What Is Visual Literacy?

While there may be different versions of the term "visual literacy," Burmark (2002) and Metros (2008) present a Constructivist interpretation of this term, as follows:

- Ability to interpret, decode, understand, and appreciate visual messages.
- Ability to create visual communications to solve problems.
- Ability to use technology to create and analyze visual communications.
- Ability to critique and analyze visual information and tools for creating visual messages.

Note that each of these involves action. As Constructivists, we must not simply observe visual messages. We must create them, interpret, analyze, and critique them. Visual literacy, much like computer literacy, is not passive.

8.2 Why Is the Visual Mode So Important?

Let us continue the computer analogy a bit longer. We all know why computers are so important today. But why the visual mode is important may not be so obvious. Researchers have identified two principal factors:

- The biological makeup of visual capabilities.
- Modern culture's dependency on the visual mode.

8.2.1 The Biological Perspective

The biological aspect makes the importance of the visual mode clear. Whereas the auditory nerve contains 30,000 to 50,000 fibers, the optic nerve contains 1 million fibers. This substantial difference in nerve fibers helps explain the powerful capabilities of the visual mode. While many people bemoan the fact that television has made everyone able (or willing) to grasp only small sound bites, research shows that, biologically, the visual mode has a huge advantage. As Constructivist teachers, we must capitalize on this knowledge. While we certainly should not rely solely on the visual mode, it is equally clear that we must not rely solely on lecture or oral instruction.

8.2.2 The Cultural Perspective

Modern culture clearly demonstrates the power of the visual mode. Metros (2008) discussed how today's culture is dependent on visual literacy. She pointed to the fact that "people make decisions based on a picture-saturated press and home-grade video" (p. 102). She reminded us that politicians conduct their campaigns through their visual image, court trials are broadcast on television, and newspapers are now fueled by charts (look at the front page of *USA Today*), graphics, and photos. Picture taking has been made more accessible through advances in technology such as image resolution, file compression, and file storage capacity. The *New York Times* recently featured an article about churches using multimedia (PowerPoint, movie clips, and the like) in sermons. And we are all aware that the cell phone has become ubiquitous and is itself being used less and less for voice communication and more and more for browsing the Internet or taking pictures, whether of an accident or a robbery in action or a visiting celebrity. No, we don't need to allow our students to use their cell phones in class, but we can make the visual mode a part of our Constructivist classroom.

8.3 Visual Aids and Constructivist Strategies

Let's consider a situation taken from a literature class. The English teacher reads the following to her class:

> Tom Sawyer faced a dilemma: it was a lovely summer morning in Saturday, and he wanted to be out wandering, singing, lazing in the sun. But instead he had to whitewash the fence: 30 yards of it, 9 feet high.

Problem 1: How to get out of the job and not get punished?

Solution 1: Get someone else to do the work.

Option 1:   His first idea: to bribe someone with a marble or some other object. But this was costly and probably would give him only a half-hour of freedom.

Option 2:   Convince other that they really wanted to do it. So, when some boys strolled by singing and joking, Tom ignored them, pretending he was so enamored with the task that he didn't notice tem. Then, "startled" by one of the boys, he carefully examined his handiwork, adding a bit of paint here and there and admiring the result. When one of the boys asked to try, Tom cleverly demurred, noting that painting the fence was a great privilege, one that his aunt wouldn't let just anyone do. He emphasized the danger if something went wrong. And in the end, he not only convinced one boy after the other to do the whitewashing, but he even got paid for it, with an apple, a kite, and such.

How can the Constructivist teacher capitalize on the visual mode to have the students examine this passage? Here is one approach.

First, she divides the class into four groups. Two groups are directed to represent Tom's situation in the form of a problem-solution graphic organizer, and the other two groups to summarize the situation using the traditional textual mode. Look at the possibilities.

Graphic Organizer Group 1.

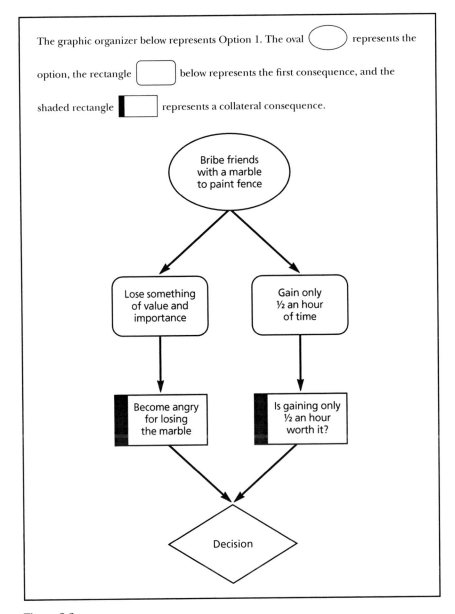

The graphic organizer below represents Option 1. The oval ◯ represents the option, the rectangle ▭ below represents the first consequence, and the shaded rectangle ▮▭ represents a collateral consequence.

Bribe friends with a marble to paint fence

Lose something of value and importance

Gain only ½ an hour of time

Become angry for losing the marble

Is gaining only ½ an hour worth it?

Decision

Figure 8.2

Graphic Organizer Group 2:   The graphic organizer shown is a visual representation of Option 2; it uses the same symbols as the first option.

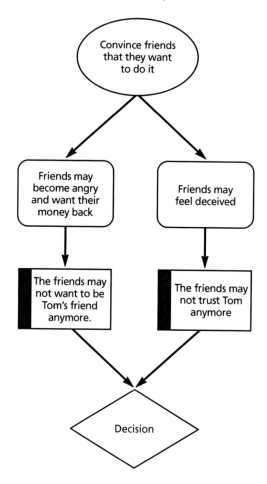

Figure 8.3

Textual Approach Group 3:   Tom could bribe his friends with a marble, but that would create a possible problem. Tom could lose something of value to him, namely, the marble. This loss would then anger Tom because he had lost something he valued, and in return he would only gain half an hour.

Textual Approach Group 4:   Tom could convince his friends that they want to do it, but he would be doing this by deceiving his friends. His friends may become angry and want their money back. They may turn on Tom because they believe that he is deceitful.

Now the teacher extends this exercise by applying the "Rattle their cage" Constructivist strategy. First, she asks the students to compare and contrast the graphical organizer results with the textual results and to respond to the following questions: Which mode is more effective? Why? Is anything lost by using the visual mode? Then she reads the actual passage, as Twain wrote it, and repeats the questions: Which is more effective? Why? Is anything lost? The students may note that tone and voice are lost in both the graphic organizers and the textual summaries.

The following example illustrates another example of using the visual mode in reading. This time, the example focuses on a much younger reading group. The story is "Goldilocks and the Three Bears." The teacher can now use another Constructivist strategy, "Turn the kaleidoscope," and have the class together fill in the chart (Figure 8.4) from the perspective of the three bears. Young children can then be asked to draw a picture representing one of the viewpoints: that of Goldilocks or that of the three bears. Refer to the chart.

Character Summary

Character _____

Sees	Does	What would I do?
The bears' house	She goes in the bears' house	
3 bowls of porridge	She eats their porridge	
3 chairs	She breaks Baby Bear's chair	
3 beds	She sleeps in Baby Bear's bed	
3 bears	She gets scared	

Figure 8.4

8.4   The Visual Mode as a Learning Tool

The visual mode has tremendous potential for the Constructivist teacher. Let's examine this.

Knowledge retention: Ives (2007) examined the effectiveness of graphic organizers for student studying systems of linear equations. One group of students received direct instruction without graphic organizers, and the other group received the same instructions but with the addition of graphic organizers. The students using graphic organizers outperformed the other group on posttests. Moreover, this group's better understanding of concepts was maintained on a posttest two to three weeks later.

Nesbit and Adesope (2006) conducted a meta-analysis of concept maps. Their study took information from 67 standardized mean difference effect sizes from 55 studies involving 5,818 participants. The results of this study indicate that the use of concept maps was linked with increased knowledge retention.

Somewhat earlier, Mayer (1989) conducted two experiments in which 34 female college students read a text about braking systems; some text contained labeled illustrations, while other text had no illustrations. The students then took tests on recall, transfer, and recognition. While labeled illustrations did not improve verbatim retention, they did help students in selective attention and in building internal connections.

Learning: Butcher (2006) investigated learning outcomes when students studied the heart and circulatory system. In these experiments the conditions were text only, text with simplified diagrams designed to put focus on important structural relations, and text with more detailed diagrams that illustrated a more accurate representation. The results showed that both types of visual representation were more effective than text only.

Even more startling were the results of a study examining the effects of concept mapping on low-achieving urban seventh graders. Guastello, Beasley, and Sinatra (2000) found that the use of concept maps with this group resulted in scores of approximately six standard deviations higher that students receiving traditional instruction.

Results with an even younger group were equally impressive. In a study by Seaman (1990), fifth-grade students were split into three groups. One group involved cooperative concept mapping, another standard concept mapping group, and the third the control. The students studied a science text and then had a weekly vocabulary test and a final. Students in both concept mapping groups outperformed the control group.

Recall: Griffin, Malone, and Kameenui (1995) studied whether graphic organizer instruction would facilitate comprehension, recall, and transfer. Their results showed that the groups receiving graphic organizer training had the highest mean scores on the immediate posttest and on the immediate recall measure. This point is important because students in this group had to learn how to construct graphic organizers as well as master the subject content that would be tested.

A few years earlier, McCagg and Dansereau (1991) conducted a study in which 81 college students participated. The results showed that knowledge mapping positively influenced student performance on recall tests. The investigators noted that the same performance was observed across two testing sessions.

Results from research also indicate that visual learning aids have been effective across languages, geographical boundaries, and content areas.

Dominant language: Graphic organizers have been shown to be effective independent of a student's dominant language. Ritchie and Gimenez (1995/1996) studied 68 fourth-grade students in a school in suburban San Diego; 31 were English-speaking students and 37 Spanish-speaking students. The results showed a statistically significant difference favoring the students using graphic organizers. The results also indicated the effectiveness of graphic organizers in computer-based instruction does not vary by the dominant language of the learner.

Geographical region: Stavridou and Kakana (2008) examined the relationship between graphic abilities and high performance in mathematics and science for students in a secondary school in northern Greece. The results from this study showed a high degree of correlation between graphic abilities and performance in both mathematics and science.

Content area: Bean et al. (1990) studied the effectiveness of combining graphical representation with an analogical study guide for high-school students studying biology concepts. The results of this study indicated that students receiving instruction that combined a pictorial representation with the study guide scored better than students who did not have access to the pictorial guide.

The strength of the visual mode was also illustrated by the work of Pribyl and Bodner (1987). Their study involved the relationship between spatial ability and performance in an organic chemistry course. In this study, students possessing high spatial scores did significantly better on questions that required an ability to apply problem-solving skills. While the study showed that spatial ability was not significant for rote memory, it did show that a high spatial ability was related to such activities as completing a reaction or manipulating two-dimensional models of molecules.

EXERCISE 8.1:
Graphical Organizers as a Summarizing Instrument

This activity uses a "fishbone" graphic organizer as both a summarizing tool and an aid for writing. The example was used for a college algebra class that had just completed studying linear functions. The instructor starts the review by showing the fishbone organizer below.

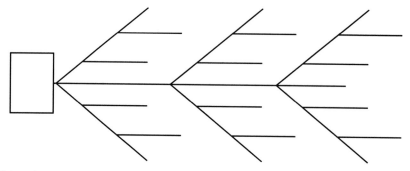

Figure 8.5

The instructor then works with students to fill out the organizer; the actual organizer for this class is shown below.

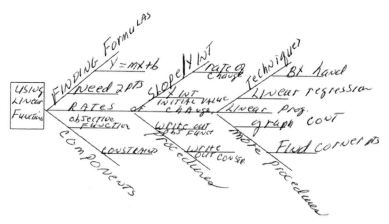

Figure 8.6

Notes: The rectangle on the left (Using linear functions) serves as the theme for a summary essay. The horizontal line in the middle contains the two main uses of linear functions: rates of change and linear programming.

Assign half the students to write an essay examining the theme of rates of change through three paragraphs: finding formulas, slope/intercept, and techniques. Assign the other half to write an essay examining the theme of linear programming supported by three paragraphs: components, procedures, and more procedures.

As an extension, different student groups can be given different formats, and the teacher can moderate a comparing and contrast discussion and a discussion of the advantages of the different formats.

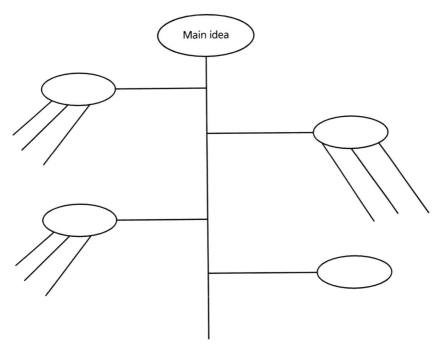

Figure 8.7

EXERCISE 8.2:
Graphical Organizers as a Time Line

Using the graphical organizer as a time line enables students to "see" a sequence of events. In this example the graphical organizer is used not only as a tool for visual knowledge but also as an activity for activating prior knowledge. The teacher starts the study of World War II by giving students a blank time line (Figure 8.8) and the dates and events below. Students then work to correctly place the dates and events on the time line.

> *Japanese expansion begins, Breakout and pursuit in France begins, Battle for Normandy, Battle of Kursk, Battle of Midway, Axis expansion in Europe, August beginning of the Eastern Front, end of the Battle of Stalingrad.*

Time line

Figure 8.8

Notes: The teacher can "Turn the kaleidoscope" and have the students write these events in a vertical list. Which is easier to understand? Why? (Do we tend to see events and dates as proceeding horizontally or vertically?)

8.5   The Visual Mode as an Assessment Tool

As Constructivist teachers, we can use concept mapping not only as learning tool for students but also as an assessment instrument. Hay, Wells, and Kinchin (2008) conducted a study in which 18 students took a pretest and created a concept map before formal instruction and, at the end of the course, took a postcourse test and created a postcourse concept map. Changes in both instruments were used to determine the amount and quality of student learning. Constructivists will notice the word "created": the students are actively involved in this assessment process.

8.6   Visual Literacy and the Arts

The Consortium of National Arts Education Associations, under the guidance of the National Committee for Standards in the Arts, has established the following national standards for arts education, including music, dance, theater, and visual arts:

1. Students use visual structures and functions of art to communicate ideas.
2. Students analyze, describe, and demonstrate how factors of time and place (such as climate, resources, ideas, and technology) influence visual characteristics that give meaning and value to a work of art.
3. Students compare characteristics of visual arts with a particular historical period or style with ideas, issues, or themes in the humanities or sciences.
4. Students reflect analytically on various interpretations as a means for understanding and evaluating works of visual art.
5. Students create multiple solutions to specific visual arts problems that demonstrate competence in producing effective relationships between structural choices and artistic functions.

These standards require students to look at "multiple solutions" and "various interpretations." The activities all are active: "communicate," "analyze," "compare," "reflect," "create." Thus, a Constructivist environment is ideally suited to meet these standards.

The standards also stress the visual mode. How can the Constructivist incorporate these standards in the classroom through the visual mode? Metzger (2007) proposed the use of historical feature films as an instrument for developing historical literacy. He cited a study indicating that 81% of 808 people responding to a survey claimed to have watched historically themed television programs and movies in the previous year. Since millions of viewers are school-age students, this medium affords a golden opportunity for shaping how they view the past. Metzger urged teachers to use historical feature films to "guide students to identify important information and ideas about the past and then to relate this knowledge to broader patterns of historical significance" (p. 68). Through carefully worded questions the teacher can help the students examine how the film is supported by available evidence, how much the film is fictionalized, and how the culture and times influenced the film. Perhaps the Constructivist teacher can supplement a history lesson on the treatment of minorities during World War II with a film such as *Children of the Camps,* documenting the U.S. internment of Japanese-Americans. What follows is an example of using historical films in the Constructivist classroom.

EXERCISE 8.3:
Using a Historical Film in Class

The teacher has the class look at a film such as *True Glory.* This documentary, released in 1945 and with an introduction by Dwight D. Eisenhower, won an Academy Award. The film describes the Allied invasion in Europe during WWII. The teacher then presents the following questions:

- How does the film align with the facts as they are presented by the text?
- What facts are presented differently by the text and the film?
- What themes are presented by the film? By the text?
- In what cultural era was the film made? How does this era influence the authenticity of the film?

After suitable discussion, the teacher then issues the following assignment:

▪ Write a letter to the film's producer outlining the discrepancies you have found. Include suggestions to make the film more authentic.

Alternatively, the teacher can ask students to find an example of artwork or music that represents the same era or situation, and compare what elements the film and that piece of art or music share.

A variation of this activity would be to have the class examine a film that is based on historical events, such as *Thirteen Days*. After viewing the film students can be put into cooperative learning groups in order to discuss the prompts that follow:

▪ What bias does the film follow?
▪ What events presented in the film are not historically correct? How does this contribute to the film's bias?
▪ If the events that were not historically correct were replaced with historically correct events, would the "artistic" value of the film be reduced? Why or why not?

Cosenza (2006) presented a similar scheme for blending the musical and visual modes. The following activity is an interpretation of her ideas from a purely pedagogical perspective.

EXERCISE 8.4:
Blending the Visual Mode with the Musical Mode

The teacher begins by discussing with the class the different types of attributes that can be used to describe artwork (mood, colors, symmetry, form, etc.).

The students work in groups of four to examine a selected piece of artwork representative of a specific time period, artist, or tradition.

Each group chooses a movement from a piece of music or a "soundscape" that captures the mood or atmosphere of the artwork.

Each group presents the work to the class and briefly explains how it fulfills the assignment.

Notes: The class then compares and contrasts the effectiveness of the visual vs. the musical mode. What is gained by the musical? Is anything lost?

8.7 Multiple Modes and Constructivism

As Constructivist teachers, we must strive to use the visual mode in conjunction with other modes. Recall Principles 5 and 7 of the Constructivist philosophy. Principle 5 states that students learn when class activities stimulate *multiple senses*; Principle 7 says that one way in which people learn is by connecting new experiences with previous experiences or by connecting previously discrete experiences to each other. Brain research indicates that visual information is stored in a separate location in the brain from that for verbal information. Since knowledge is constructed by connecting different locations together, effective teaching must connect the visual mode to other modes.

Mautone and Mayer (2007) conducted a study in which some students were shown cognitive aids prior to viewing four geography graphs; other students were not. Some students also received signaling as an instructional aid; signaling refers to words and cues that make given information more prevalent, for example, using headings, outlines, highlighting, or numbered lists. All of the students in the study were asked to write a summary of the important information presented by the graphs. The results indicated that combining signaling and concrete graphic organizers produced an increase in both relational and causal statements. These results show the power of using multiple modes.

EXERCISE 8.5:
Multiple Modes in the Mathematics Classroom

Let's say the class is studying isosceles triangles. The approach is to have the students explain the theorem using four different modes:

- Say it in words.
- Write it using different words.
- Say it symbolically.
- Give an example by using appropriate diagrams.

Here are some results.

- *Say it in words*
  John: When a triangle has two sides with the same length, it will have two angles equal in measure.
- *Write it using different words*
  Sue: When you have a triangle with two congruent angles, you will have those opposite angles congruent.
- *Say it symbolically.*

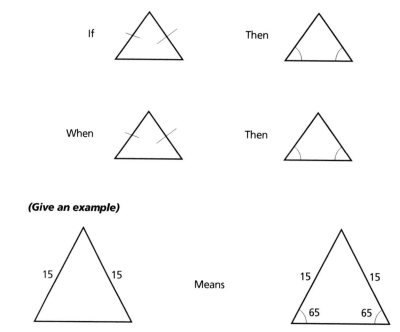

Figure 8.9

Now the teacher applies the Constructivist strategy of "rattling their cage," by putting the following on the board and asking the students what the measures of the other angles are.

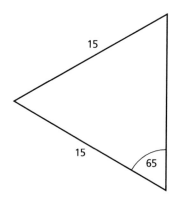

Figure 8.10

8.8   Levels of Visual Constructivism

Alesandrini (2002) examined four levels of visual Constructivism. Each of the levels refers to the mode of the instruction and the mode of the student response. Three of the four levels involve the visual mode:

- Verbal Instruction-Visual Constructivism.
- Visual Instruction-Verbal Constructivism.
- Visual Instruction-Visual Constructivism.

The remaining activities in this chapter demonstrate how to put Alesandrini's levels into practice in a Constructivist classroom.

EXERCISE 8.6:
Verbal Instruction to Visual Student Product: Assessment Course in Education

The teacher delivers a lecture on the concept of a standard score (standardized tests represent their results with standard scores).

The teacher then asks students to work in groups of three or four to create for parents a web page that explains the meaning of a standard score.

Notes: Alternately, students can design a one-page fact sheet explaining what a standard score is.

EXERCISE 8.7:
Verbal Instruction to Visual Student Product: Designing a Historical Monument

Duraisingh and Mansilla (2007) described a project in which students design a monument or memorial to an event, theme, group, or person relevant to the study. While Duraisingh and Mansilla focused on a history class, the project can easily be used in other classes: from science (Mendel), music (atonality), and economics (the stock market crash), and even physical education (the dolphin kick). The following activities seek to blend the ideas and themes of Duraisingh and Mansilla with Constructivist strategies.

1. The teacher uses cooperative learning, Constructivist questioning, and authentic writing to show students how monuments represent a unique way to focus on important historical events and people. The teacher suggests several events, people, or groups that the students may choose from to create a monument.
2. The students conduct historical research in order to create different interpretations.

3. Students present two design choices to the class for discussion and comparison/contrast.

4. Students prepare and present their final design.

<u>EXERCISE 8.8:</u>

Visual Instruction to Verbal Constructivism: Using Illustrations to Help Teach Reading

The teacher asks student the following questions:

- Let's start the story by looking at the cover. What do you predict the story is about?
- Look at the picture of _____. Is _____ happy or sad? Why do you say this?
- How will the story end? What makes you say this?
- How would you make this picture of _____ better? What would you change in this picture? Why?
- How would you change the ending of the story? Why?

Notes: The use of visuals to support reading can also be used in guided reading. The Constructivist teacher can ask the following questions:

- Which pictures helped you understand the problem?
- Which pictures helped with the setting?
- Did you find any of the pictures misleading? Which illustrations would you change to help you learn information about the story better?

<u>EXERCISE 8.9:</u>

Visual Instruction to Verbal Constructivism: Using Video Games for Motivating Descriptive Writing

Hutchison (2007) discussed the blending of descriptive writing and video games. This activity is an adaptation of Hutchison's ideas. The teacher brings in a video game (preferably one the students are unlikely to be familiar with), mentions the target audience, and demonstrates the game. The teacher then tells the students:

- You have just started your new job as a writer for *Modern Video Games Magazine*. You are to write a one-page review of this game.

■ Included in this review you are to address the following: Is the game suited for the audience? What suggestions can you make for improving the visuals?

EXERCISE 8.10:
Visual Instruction to Visual Constructivism: Teacher Methods Course in Education

Students watch a feature film on education (e.g., *Stand and Deliver, Mr. Holland's Opus*). The teacher then divides the class into groups. Each group selects a teacher in the film and *creates a graphics organizer* depicting the methods used by that teacher.

Notes: Have the groups present their results to the entire class and compare and contrast the methods used by the different teachers.

EXERCISE 8.11:
Visual Instruction to Visual Constructivism: Designing a Magazine Cover

Magazines fill our newsstands, targeted to specific audiences ranging from the very young (*Ranger Rick*) to the retiree (*AARP*). The teacher brings in appropriate magazines for students to discuss layouts, pictures, graphics, headings, fonts, and so on.

Students work in groups to create a "template" for creating a new magazine cover for the targeted audience. The template will include the following:

■ Recurring themes among headings.
■ Recurring themes among images.
■ How themes and headings connect with purpose of the magazine.

Students must defend their template orally. Each group creates a magazine cover, based on feedback from the other groups and the teacher.

9

Visual Literacy: Why It Works

$\mathbf{I}$n Chapter 8 we focused on the many places where graphic organizers work and from learning to recalling, from reading to mathematics to history. But one might wonder why visual organizers are so effective. Cognitive learning theories provide insight into the reasons these graphic aids work.

One answer might be that graphic organizers help in *making new connections* between ideas. People who use these aids have to identify salient themes or properties or components and then fit them in some kind of logical relationship, a flow chart, say. The act of placing them on such a graphic organizer, seeing the connecting lines or concentric circles trigger ideas that simply putting items in a list may not.

Two studies support this idea. Alvermann (1981) studied tenth graders who read an expository passage. His results showed that graphic organizers were significant when students were required to reorganize information. Since the reorganization of information is a Constructivist activity, this is essential information for the Constructivist teacher. More recently, a study by Harpaz, Balik, and Ehrenfeld (2004) focused on concept mapping in nursing education. The researchers reported that the students believed

The Comprehensive Handbook of Constructivist Teaching, pages 109–117
Copyright © 2010 by Information Age Publishing
All rights of reproduction in any form reserved.

that concept mapping encouraged independent thinking, improved their ability in making connections between different areas, and increased their confidence in applying knowledge in clinical work. Their article also reported that teachers believed that concept mapping helped in integrating material and enabled students to become active learners. Again, that word "active"—a key Constructivist concept.

9.1   Organizing and Reorganizing Information

Hyerle (2004) reminds us that 70% of the body's sensory receptors are contained in the eyes and "that when teachers use visuals in the classroom to represent concepts, their students retain them longer" (p. xl). He noted that the brain "seeks patterns of information to network" (p. 23). Burmark (2002) reported on research done by the 3M Corporation indicating that people can process information in the visual mode 60,000 times more quickly than information in the textual mode. A quick Internet search comes up with many types of visual organizers that teachers can use to have students organize and reorganize knowledge in the visual mode.

EXERCISE 9.1:
Using a Map to Compare Vice-Presidential Candidates

Both former governor Palin and Vice President Biden were known for having occasional difficulty expressing themselves. But they differed strongly in their ideas about the role of the vice president (energy advisor, active campaigner for disabled vs. helping the president in a more passive, supportive role).

The teacher can ask students to create a graphic organizer to indicate these points. The teacher can engage students in a discussion or ask students to complete a written assignment that examines whether the chosen visual clarifies the differences.

9.2   Constructing Knowledge

While visual organizers present an exciting opportunity for the Constructivist teacher, Simmons, Griffin, and Kameenui (1988) raised a "yellow flag." They investigated and compared using teacher-constructed graphic organizers before text reading and after text reading and after text reading and using a traditional form of instruction that involved frequent questions and discussion focused on the text. Their results indicated that the graphic organizer treatments did *not* prove more effective than traditional instruction for comprehension and retention of science information by sixth-grade students. Can you hypothesize why?

One possible explanation is that the students were not the *constructors* of the graphic organizers. As the Constructivist philosophy advocates, real knowledge is the result of the learner's constructing it. Graphic organizers by themselves do not create knowledge. The teacher must create a Constructivist environment for the students to do their own creating.

But there is also indication that students can and should *interact* with these organizers in other ways, besides simply creating them. Robinson et al. (2006) conducted a study in which students worked with either partially completed graphic organizers (that they had to complete) or fully completed organizers. The results showed that students working with the partially completed graphic organizers scored higher on quizzes than did the other students. That may, at first may, seem counterintuitive: do students work better with half a study guide? But active interaction with visual organizers is better than passive use of the organizers.

Chang, Sung, and Chen (2002) came to a similar conclusion in a study involving 126 fifth graders. Their results indicated that map-correction activities were the most effective in enhancing text comprehension and summarization. In this type of activity, students interacted with a map that was approximately 40% incorrect. Correcting the organizers, like filling in partially completed ones, required the students to actively participate in the learning process.

We now have several ideas for our Constructivist classroom.

- Wherever possible, use graphic organizers as part of cooperative learning.
- Have students compare and contrast their graphic organizers.
- Have students use graphic organizers in conjunction with other modes.
- Include in graphic organizer activities the generation of organizers, the correction of organizers, and the completion of partially filled out organizers.

Now, let's put these ideas into practice.

EXERCISE 9.2:
Generating and Comparing Organizer Activities

This exercise is adopted from a Measurement and Evaluation class. The lesson is on standard scores and statistics. Before formal instruction, students are given a piece of paper with the following words on it:

median, mode, standard deviation, percentiles, range, distribution, standard score, normal distribution, mean, deviations, spread.

The students are then given the following partially completed graphic organizer below and are given formal instruction about the terms.

The students are told that there are mistakes in the organizer, and they are asked to complete the organizer where there are question marks.

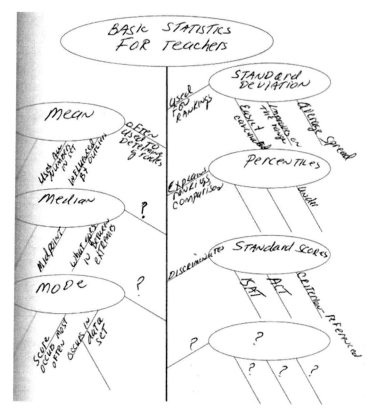

Figure 9.1

Students then compare their corrections and additions with each other. This activity can be done during or after instruction.

9.3 Putting It Together: Combining the Visual Mode with the Constructivist Strategies

The following is a series of four projects that you can use that combine graphic organizers with four of the Constructivist strategies presented earlier in the book. The projects are based on the movie *Twilight*, but you can substitute something else from literature or a film class.

EXERCISE 9.3:
Analyzing a Movie Using Graphic Organizers

The class watches the movie *Twilight*.

> *Project 1.* Using the Strategy "Captain of their own ship"
> In the movie *Twilight* neither Bella nor Edward fits in with the crowd. Each student must create a graphic organizer comparing the two characters. The students then compare their choices and defend their selection.
>
> *Project 2.* Using the Strategy "Turn the kaleidoscope"
> Each student creates a graphic organizer for the same assignment, only this time showing the conflict that arises between Edward and James.
>
> *Project 3.* Using the Strategy "TV Reality show"
> The students create a graphic organizer to illustrate a major struggle faced by the characters in their relationship, for example, how Edward is drawn by the primal pull of Bella's scent, yet struggles to suppress his need because of his love for her.
>
> *Project 4.* Using the Strategy "Rattle their cage"
> The students organize in pairs. One student creates an incorrectly filled out graphic organizer. The other student corrects it.

9.4 PowerPoint

PowerPoint presentations have become as much of an American tradition as apple pie and baseball. Most of us have used such presentations in the classroom. But is there some special relationship between PowerPoint presentations and Constructivism? Or should we even be using PowerPoint in a Constructivist environment? Putting it another way, do PowerPoint slides create or interfere with a Constructivist approach?

9.4.1 Challenges and Limitations

A decade ago, Shaw, Brown, and Bromily (1998) found PowerPoint limiting. They particularly criticized the bullet lists that are so popular; they believed that leaving out the narratives between the bullet points leaves out the assumptions and possible analysis by the students.

Parks (1999) also raised some warning notes. In teaching several sections on macroeconomics, Parks acknowledged that PowerPoint enabled him to become more organized, and these had a positive influence on students; however, he stated that the slides "can be a very passive (and hence negative) teaching device" (p. 209).

Like Parks, Reinhardt (1999) reported that her classes felt that Power-Point presentations provided advantages such as being easy to read, keeping the lectures more organized, and helping them clarify information. However, she also found that the bullet slides may not be necessarily stimulating and that some students felt that they became passive spectators. Tufte (2003) was stronger in his criticisms; he described PowerPoint as "entirely present-er-oriented, and not content-oriented, not audience-oriented" (p. 4).

9.4.2 Making Visual Aids Interactive

These studies indicate that PowerPoint presentations can have mixed results. One way you can address this situation is to examine the Construc-tivist strategies we've presented in the earlier chapters. As an educator, you can analyze whether a PowerPoint presentation will enable students to be autonomous, allow for subjective interpretation and creation ("Captain of their own ship"), be used in an authentic platform ("TV reality show"), or enable the student to make connections ("Turn the kaleidoscope" and "Rattle their cages"). Meltzer (2000) encouraged teachers to *not* allow stu-dents to use clip art when doing projects. She believes that students learn more by creating images from scratch; this mandate can easily be applied to PowerPoint presentations.

Gautreau (2004) presented ideas for an interactive multimedia presenta-tion. She advocated the hyperlinks to ensure that a PowerPoint presentation is nonlinear; by having students create different possible hyperlinks and then write reflections on them, a Constructivist environment is created. Other pos-sibilities include having student groups compare each other's hyperlinks.

The following activity is a bit different from the ones presented thus far in this handbook. Rather than an exercise to be done in class by the students, the activity is intended for you, to help you evaluate your Power-Point slides.

EXERCISE 9.4:
Analysis of a PowerPoint Presentation

Look at the presentation that follows. It represents a short presentation on Formative assessment. The teacher would present the slides in the tradi-tional, lecture format with the students taking notes.

Formative Assessment: Definition and Purpose

- Assessment that is used to monitor learning progress
- The purpose of formative assessment is to provide feedback to the teacher and to the student concerning the student's progress

Examples of Formative Assessment

- Rough drafts of essays
- Practice tests and Practice quizzes
- Teacher observation of students during class activities

Formative Assessment and Grading

- The purpose of formative is to improve learning and teaching
- Thus, the results are NOT usually used for assigning grades

Formative Assessment: Summary

- Monitors progress
- Provides feedback
- Rough drafts, practice tests, and quizzes
- Usually, grades are not assigned

Figure 9.2

Now, let's look at and analyze how a Constructivist teacher would use PowerPoint Presentation for the same topic.

Formative Assessment: Definition

- Let's consider some examples of assessment that have been used in this class: rough drafts, practice tests, and journal entries.
- These are examples of formative assessment.
- Using these examples as background information, write down your definition of formative assessment.
- Be prepared for a pair/share.

Figure 9.3

In this slide, students are being made "Captain of their ship"; also, with the Pair/Share, they have the possibility of having "their cage rattled."

Let's examine the next two slides and see the Constructivist strategies that they use.

Examples of Formative Assessment from Other Classes

- Think of three other examples of formative assessment from other classes you have taken.
- Write these down and rank them, from most effective to least effective.

Formative Assessment Outside the Classes

- Consider two examples of formative assessment at your job or in some outside activity.
- Write these down.
- Get with your group and pick out the best two from your group.
- Be prepared to have one student put these on the board.
- As a class, we will put your answers into categories.

Figure 9.4

Both of these slides are empowering students to "Be Captain of Their Ship." The group sharing, the rankings, and the sharing on the board provide opportunities to "Rattle their Cage," and "Turn the Kaleidoscope."

In using the next slide, the Constructivist teacher has the students use their texts, and then uses the slides to present Constructivist activities.

Formative Assessment and Grades

- Let's go to page _____ of your text.
- Find the passage that discusses the relationship between grading and formative assessment.
- Do you agree or disagree?
- Be prepared to defend your answer.

Figure 9.5

In the final slide the instructor passes out a graphical organizer that they must fill out; this can be done individually or with another person. Students then compare their organizers with another student's and then must write a short essay explaining what they learned from the organizer of other students.

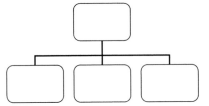

Formative Assessment Summary

- Below is a graphical organizer.

- Work with your partner to fill out the organizer and to summarize our discussion on Formative assessment.
- After this is completed, compare your organizer with another group's.
- What have you learned from the other groups?

Figure 9.6

EXERCISE 9.5:
Making PowerPoint More Interactive

Of course, PowerPoint offers far more than mere static bullets. As a Constructivist activity, you can have students redesign a slide. As an example, consider a lesson on how to solve a simple Soduku puzzle. Bullet points might be used to suggest starting in the left square and determining which numbers are messing. Then the students might suggest how to enliven this, for example, by suddenly highlighting the numbers you were pointing to in the rest of the column or row that you couldn't use.

10

Macrostrategies for Creating a Constructivist Environment

The Bridging Question Strategy

While Chapters 5 through 8 focus on activities that emphasize a certain mode, the Constructivist teacher will always blend the main modality with other modalities when the opportunity presents itself. We focus here on *macrostrategies*—Constructivist activities that include different modes and have different components. The first of the macrostrategies is that of the Bridging Question Strategy (BQS). This chapter is adapted from one of my articles that appeared in the fall 2007 edition of the *Journal for the Practical Application of Constructivist Theory in Education.*

10.1 Making Connections

Let's review some concepts concerning the creation of new knowledge. As Learning Principle 7 states, people learn by connecting new experiences to previous knowledge. Leinhardt (1992) commented on this view when she wrotes: "The impact of prior knowledge is not a matter of 'readiness,' com-

---

ponent skills, or exhaustiveness; it is an issue of depth, interconnectedness, and access" (p. 22). As a secondary math teacher, I have found that making connections is more than an "aha!" moment of remembering something; rather, it is an integrated *process* of making two experiences interconnect in scope and organization. "Readiness" implies a static state; "activation" involves ensuring that students can actively build on a network of ideas.

Bartlett (1997), a specialist in memory, stated the following concerning the act of remembering: "It is an imaginative reconstruction, or construction, built out of the relation of our attitude towards a whole active mass of organised past reactions or experience" (p. 213). Note the use of the words "reconstruction" and "construction." What is involved here is far more than mere recall of prior knowledge. Like a true Constructivist, Bartlett viewed "remembering" as involving continuous action for knowledge creation.

This continuous action of connecting prior knowledge with new experiences requires intense effort. John Dewey (1991) said that the process involves "following up and linking together the specific suggestions that specific things arouse" (p. 39). New knowledge does not just occur.

Saxe (1985) emphasized that the prior knowledge activated should be something that people have experienced on a regular basis. He examined the effect of Western schooling on the Oksapmin children of Papua New Guinea. These children used a culturally developed arithmetical system of using body parts to solve problems. Saxe explored how they would use this system to solve new problems presented by Western culture. He found that the Oksapmin children did develop new techniques to solve new problems, but these new techniques were the offspring of their previous knowledge. The work of Saxe indicates that an effective type of prior knowledge to activate is the type indigenous to one's everyday life.

The theme of knowledge connection as a process is also emphasized by brain researchers. Diamond and Hopson (1998), for example, examined knowledge as the result of a process involving cells and neurons. They envisioned neurons and cells migrating up vertical stems. The cells, in the migration process, hop off at the right point, and form a layer; then the next group comes up, migrates through this existing layer, and forms a new one above it (p. 44). Their work provides a biological foundation to the activity of connecting new experiences to prior experiences.

This finding can now be applied to the challenge facing all teachers. Anyone who has taught mathematics has heard comments like "I am smart, but not math smart" or "I am a good student, except in math" or "My daughter is extremely smart, except in math class, and that is because math is hard for everyone." Such comments seem to indicate that mathematical and academic thinking and ordinary thinking are radically different, separated by a large gap. However, our previous discussion and the work of Saxe indicate that this may not necessarily be true.

Almost half a century ago, Vygotsky (1962) argued that academic knowledge and everyday knowledge should be connected to each other. Vygotsky believed that there are two types of knowledge, spontaneous knowledge and scientific knowledge. *Spontaneous knowledge* is knowledge that the student constructs in his everyday experience, while *scientific knowledge* is knowledge that the student constructs through direct, formal instruction. Vygotsky argued that spontaneous knowledge and scientific knowledge—though different in their nature, construction, and development—should not be kept separate. He criticized Piaget for "failing to see the interaction between the two kinds of concepts and the bonds that unite them into a total system of concepts in the course of the child's intellectual development" (p. 84). Vygotsky viewed the two concepts as informing each other and working toward each other:

> We believe that the two processes, the development of spontaneous and of nonspontaneous concepts, are related and constantly influence each other. They are parts of a single process: the development of concept formation, which is affected by varying external and internal conditions but is essentially a unitary process. (p. 85)

Vygotsky thus presented a case for a dynamic equilibrium between formal academic knowledge and the everyday knowledge of people.

Vygotsky's ideas have been supported by other research. For example, Osman and Hannafin (1994) discuss the concept of "orienting questions." Orienting questions can be thought of as questions or ideas that are *concept-related* to an upcoming topic but are not necessarily *content-related*. As an example, they discussed how the tossing of a coin two times is related to the probability of inheriting genetic traits. Like Vygotsky, Osman and Hannafin presented the idea of using everyday knowledge (coin tossing) to help students learn a content topic (genetic inheritance) that is conceptually related to it.

These studies led me to develop the bridging question strategy for Constructivist teachers.

10.2   The Bridging Question Strategy

The bridging question strategy (BQS) is a teaching strategy that involves connecting everyday, manifest knowledge to an academic concept the students are learning. In reference to some activity, one asks, "What is going on here?" The desired answer is not a simple description of the particular activity; rather, it is an abstraction of the specific to the general. Wrapping and unwrapping a package can be used as a bridge to concepts used in solving equations. Deciding on what new car to buy can be related or bridged to classifying polygons. The activity of taking money from one account and putting it in another is analogous to the translation of a conic.

10.2.1 Implementing the Bridging Question

The Bridging Question Strategy consists of three phases.

1. Present a bridging activity to bring the concepts of interest into focus.
2. Fully activate the bridging question. This can be done as follows:
   - Break the class into groups, and have the groups compare responses to the bridging question.
   - Express responses to the bridging question in different modes, or words.
   - Have the groups develop their own questions based on the above activities.
3. Bridge to the more remote mathematical concept. This can be done as follows:
   - Have students predict how the bridging question is related to the more remote mathematical concepts.
   - Lead them (if necessary) to understand the connection between the bridging question and the more remote concepts.
   - Present the more remote concepts, and then discuss with students how the bridging question and these are related.

10.2.2 Example of Using the BQS

Let's look at how we can use the BQS to help students learn the concept of reversing a mathematical process. We'll use the everyday experience of wrapping and unwrapping a package. This is analogous to one method used in solving equations, but it can be related to both simpler and more complex mathematical processes.

Present the bridging activity

We begin by having one student volunteer to wrap the package and another write the steps on the board.

a. Put the present inside the box (photo A).
b. Close the box (photo B).

c. Put the box on the paper (photo C).

d. Fold the paper and add nametag (photo D).

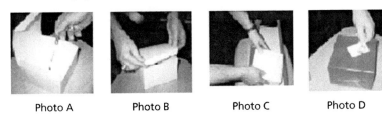

| Photo A | Photo B | Photo C | Photo D |

Figure 10.1

Now we have that student or another student unwrap the package. Again, the steps are written on the board. The board should read as follows:

Wrapping the Package	Unwrapping the Package
Put the present inside the box	Take off the name tag and unfold paper
Close the box	Take box out of paper
Put the box on the paper	Open the box
Fold the paper and add name tag	Take out present

We have activated the concept of *undoing operations in reverse order.* While some students may see this immediately, maybe it is necessary to coach others to see that the two processes undo each other in reverse order.

At this juncture some students may already recognize that the process of wrapping and unwrapping a package is analogous to solving equations. Others will not. The next phase will clarify the analogy.

Fully activate the bridging question

The students are split the students into groups. Each group discusses the relationship between the wrapping and unwrapping processes and then write down their findings. Then each group presents their findings.

Next, each group must construct their own example of two activities that "undo each other in reverse order." Again, each group present their findings. Students may come up with concepts such as leaving the house, getting in the car, and pulling out of the driveway (compared to the process of coming home in the evening) and coming into a classroom, getting out one's homework, and opening the text. In both cases the students are activating and strengthening the concept of undoing an operation in reverse order.

Bridge to the more remote mathematical concept

Students who can correctly read an equation can try to predict how the "undoing processes in reverse order" concept relates to solving equations. Most likely, however, the teacher will need review with the class the concept of the order of operations.

$$3x^2 \cdot +5 = y$$

Let $x = 2$
Squaring gives $x^2 = 4$
Multiplying by 3 gives $x^2 \cdot 3 = 12$
Adding 5 gives $x^2 \cdot 3 + 5 = 17$

Figure 10.2

In this example we have squared, multiplied, and then added. A few more examples of the order of operations will solidify this sequence. The teacher must then coach the students to apply the recently activated concept of undoing operations in reverse order. We suggest putting the following on the board:

Order of Operations	Solving Equations
Exponents	Undo exponents
Multiplication/division	Undo multiplication/division
Addition/subtraction	*Undo addition/subtraction*

We now apply the process of undoing in reverse order.

➢ Begin with the equation: $x^2 \cdot 3 + 5 = 17$.

➢ Since addition was done last, undo the addition of 5, giving: $x^2 \cdot 3 = 12$.

➢ Since multiplication was done next to last, undo the multiplication by 3, giving: $x^2 = 4$.

➢ Undo the squaring of x by taking the square root, giving: $x = 2$.

Figure 10.3

The teacher should have each group compare and contrast the process of wrapping/unwrapping with that of solving equations.

10.2.3 BQS and Classification

The bridging question strategy is not limited to secondary math classes. Let's look at how it can be used to help students understand the importance and significance of classifying items. Classification is always a challenge to teach because students view this lesson as uninteresting. The BQS can change this by increasing student engagement, which in turn increases deeper understanding of the process of classifying triangles.

Present the bridging activity.

The students are given two sheets depicting cars and trucks. The students are asked to rank the vehicles in order from most desirable to least desirable.

Figure 10.4

Fully activate the bridging question/ Bridge to the more general mathematical concept.

Next, the students go to the board and discuss and defend their rankings. Most likely, students will disagree about the rankings. The teacher can use this opportunity to ask the students why they disagree. The students should create the following important classification concept: Classification (ranking) is an arbitrary concept that depends on the foundation for the classification (e.g., cost, sportiness, durability).

Then, the students continue with the activation by asking them to classify five poems (they can be rhymed or not, or cover different subjects, or be humorous or serious, for example). The assignment can be expressed as something that the editor of their text wants to do in order to make the poetry unit seem more coherent.

Starting with the everyday concept of classification of cars, the students have bridged to the abstract concept of classification. The students may well find that poetry has suddenly become more interesting!

In the remainder of this chapter, we present two more exercises, both using the BGS, in a history class and a reading class, for high-school students and elementary-school students, respectively. The activities show the broad applicability of this Constructivist activity.

EXERCISE10.1:
BQS in a History/Social Studies Class

The BQS can be applied to the study of conflicts between governments or ideologies. Such conflicts can be viewed in terms of winners and losers. By activating a manifest experience from the students' life, the teacher can use Constructivist teaching activities to bridge to the wider perspective of winning in war.

For a specific example, consider World War II. While on the surface it appears as if the Allies won the war, the historian Richard Overy (1995) reminds us of a broader perspective:

> When people heard that the title of my next book was to be "Why the Allies Won", it often provoked the retort: "Did they?" There are many ways of winning. With the passage of time it has become possible to argue that none of the three major Allies-Britain, the United States and the Soviet Union-won a great deal. Britain lost her empire and her leading world role; the United States that they traded one European enemy for another.

Overy's quote points out that the concept of winning is complex. In teaching about World War II, the teacher must activate the thinking necessary to understand a concept such as winning a war.

One way in which a teacher can do this is through a class discussion of immediate (or, apparent) and eventual consequences. For example, the teacher can relate how he and a friend liked the same girl. The girl chose him, but in the end he lost a friend.

Notes: Another example could be choosing to go to dinner with a business associate on the day you were supposed to go out with a friend or spouse or relative. In accordance with the BQS, a teacher must coach students to "dig deep under the surface." This example can readily be applied to an economics class when studying business takeovers.

EXERCISE 10.2:
Example from a Kindergarten Reading Class

In this example, the concept of finding what fits the best is bridged to what book is best to read.

The teacher asks the students what shoes a child should wear. In terms of fit, a child cannot wear his father's shoes because the shoes are too big. The teacher can coach the students to connect this idea to the concept of developmental fit.

Next, the teacher asks students whether they would wear a ballerina's shoes to go fishing; this concept can be bridged to the concept of determining the *purpose of reading*. To make the bridging more concrete, the teacher can bring in examples of different shoes or can bring in pictures of shoes.

Now, to bridge to the concept of *choosing the correct book,* the teacher can review the story of Goldilocks and the Three Bears. The mother bear's porridge wasn't right, and the papa bear's porridge wasn't right, but he baby bear's porridge was just right.

GOLDILOCKS RULE

Too easy	Just right	Too hard
I know all the rules	I understand	I do not know a lot of words
It does not make me think	It makes me think	I do not understand

Figure 10.5

10.3 More than Metaphor

The BQS is a Constructivist macrostrategy that is effective for all ages and all content areas. It is more than using a metaphor to teach. It is a process of activating manifest or spontaneous knowledge. The BQS consists of many Constructivist activities in order to enable us to connect noncontent concepts to a new concept being taught.

11

Creating a Constructivist Environment by Using Kinesthetic Activities, Manipulatives, and Drama

Our journey to being a Constructivist teacher now takes us to the examination of manipulatives, kinesthetic learning, and drama. Let's start by considering a class in trigonometry where the teacher wants to use the trig ratios to determine the effect of the wind on an airplane. We'll assume that students can already use the basic trigonometric ratios to solve for unknown lengths and angle measures. The students are supposed to determine by how many degrees the plane will be off course. We will examine two scenarios.

Scenario 1

Teacher: Good morning, class. Today we will be studying forces and vectors. A vector is a directed line segment; it has magnitude and direction. Let me draw examples on the board.

The Comprehensive Handbook of Constructivist Teaching, pages 129–146

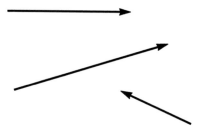

Figure 11.1

Teacher: What can you tell me about the vectors?

Student A: Well, I guess that vectors can go in any direction and can be of any size?

Teacher: That is correct. Now, when two forces act on each other, there is a resultant vector, not surprisingly called the "resultant." Look at my diagram.

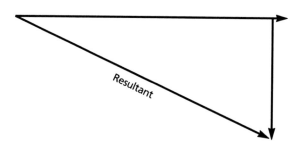

Figure 11.2

Teacher: Are there any questions?

Student B: How did you know to connect them like you did?

Teacher: We always connect the end of one with the beginning of the other.

Teacher: Now, let's suppose that a plane is headed due east at 230 mph and there is a wind from the north at 48 mph. How many degrees will the plane be off course? What shall we do? Let's start with our diagram.

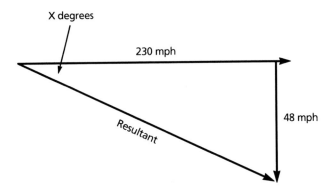

Figure 11.3

Teacher: Now let's use a trig equation to solve for x degrees.

The above scenario illustrates the method that many of us encountered. Now, let's look at Scenario 2, which depicts how a Constructivist teacher would use kinesthetic learning ("hands on") to teach the same lesson.

Scenario 2
Teacher: Let's look at the following situation:

A plane is flying due west at 200 mph (this is referred to as the "heading"). There is a wind from the north at 50 mph. Determine how many degrees the plane will be off course (called the "drift angle").

Teacher: Let's do a "know, need to know" approach. First the easy part: What do we know? [The teacher can expect a quick show of hands and can quickly write the results on the board.]

Teacher: Great. Now, what do we need to know?
[The teacher then calls on students and creates the chart below.]

Know	Need to Know
1. The plane is headed east	1. The drift angle
2. The plane flies at 200 mph	2. How the wind can actually push a plane off course[a]
3. The wind is from the north at 50 mph	

---

[a] There is usually a big discussion on this, so the following activity is used to examine this.

> **Teacher:** We want to look at what the effects will be in this situation. You will divide into pairs and perform the experiment below three different times. Remember: Look at all the pictures and read the explanations before you attempt the experiment.
>
> a. Draw a line that goes from right to left. AT THE SAME TIME, your partner will pull the paper straight down. You will do this two times. The first time your partner will pull the paper at a rate greater than the rate you are drawing the line. The second time your partner will pull the paper at a rate slower than the rate you are drawing the line.

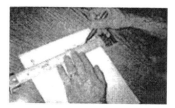

Figure 11.4

Figure 11.5

> b. After this you will compare your results/drawing with that of other groups.

The teacher now has each group put their diagrams on the board; most groups have something that looks like the diagram below.

Figure 11.6

Teacher: Good. Now I want each group write down, in one sentence, what this experiment has to do with the problem of the effect of wind on the plane.

Teacher: Okay, now let's try to come up with a consensus. Get in groups of four to discuss one another's sentence. Again, what has this experiment to do with the wind and the plane. That is, what do the two people represent—the one drawing and the one pulling? [The following are typical responses.]

1. The person drawing the line represents the plane.
2. The person pulling the paper represents the wind.
3. The wind pushes the plane off its course.
4. The plane is pulled off course, going southwest instead of due west.

Teacher: After reading what each group has put up on the board, we can agree that the wind can push a plane off course; in this case the plane is pushed toward a southwest course.

Now, each one of you has been given a ruler and a protractor. Get with your partner, and discuss what we can do to find the drift angle. You will want to use a scale drawing. What scale should we use? Should we use feet, inches, meters? Work with your partner on this.

After a class discussion the consensus often reached is to use a scale of 1 cm = 20 mph. This discussion is important because it provides students with the opportunity to connect or bridge the problem to the visual representation. It is essential that students work with one another to develop a scale so the diagram will fit onto the page; by doing this they become "Captain of their own ship." The teacher can do this through cooperative groups and then can lead the class in a discussion in order to reach a consensus. The students then draw the scale diagrams shown by the figures(1 cm = 10 mph). The path of the plane flying east at 200 mph is represented by a segment 10 cm in length, and the wind is represented by a segment vertical segment 5 cm in length.

Figure 11.7

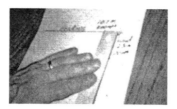

Figure 11.8

> **Teacher:** Now measure the drift angle with your protractor, and discuss your answers with one another.

Figure 11.9

The teacher then has the students do a few problems using this scale drawing approach. When the teacher is confident that students understand the problems through the kinesthetic/visual, he will then bridge to solving the problems with trigonometry.

> **Teacher:** You've measured the angle on the scale drawing with your protractor, but this can become very tedious. Is there an easier way to do this? [The teacher can expect a mixed reaction; some students will immediately connect this approach to solving through trigonometry, while others will not. This problem can be solved by the using the tangent function and its inverse It is for these "others" that the teacher must provide the opportunity to make this vital connection.]

> **Teacher:** Let's see if we can find another way to solve these types of problems. Let's look at the following problems. The teacher then puts the following problems and diagrams on the board and prepares to lead a discussion on how to solve these problems with trigonometry.

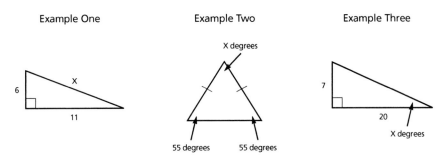

Figure 11.10

The purpose of the following activity is to have students create the idea of using the tangent ratio and its inverse to solve this problem. This can be done by looking at different techniques that students already know and connect them to the present problem. The diagrams above represent a small sampling of the problems that should be used; the teacher assigns each group of two students to discuss (a) how their problem differs from the aviation problem and (b) how they would solve the problem. Student groups come to the board to explain their reasoning. Example One differs from the aviation problem because Example One gives the lengths of both legs and is solving for the length of the hypotenuse, and the aviation problem is looking to solve for one of the acute angles. Example Two differs from the aviation problem in that it does not contain a right angle. Example Three provides the length of two legs of the triangle and is looking to solve for one of the acute angles. Through discussing and comparing the examples with the aviation problem, students can connect to the use of the trigonometric ratios to solve the problem.

> **Teacher:** Okay, we are now ready to compare the answers from the two methods.

1. Are the answers the same?
2. What surprised you about the lesson?
3. Is there anything you are still unsure about?
4. Did the activity help you learn?

Scenario 2 demonstrates the characteristics of "Captain of your ship," "Creating a TV reality show," "Rattling their cage," and "Turning the kaleidoscope"— all fine Constructivist activities. It also features the theme of this chapter: using the *kinesthetic mode* in a Constructivist environment. The rest of the chapter examines this theme, using the element of role playing.

11.1 Terminology

For this chapter, "kinesthetic" will refer to any type of bodily movement responding to visual, auditory, or tactile activity. A "manipulative" is defined as any object that a person can handle or move in order to use the senses to examine a topic. For the Constructivist teacher, using the body and manipulatives provides another avenue for processing and creating new knowledge.

11.2 What Educational Theory and Research Say

The concept of using the kinesthetic mode is not new in education. Piaget's cognitive development theory assumes that the origin of mental operations is rooted in kinesthetic experiences. Bruner (1967) believed that knowledge can be represented in three ways: enactive, iconic, and symbolic. He described enactive representation as a "set of actions appropriate for achieving a certain result" (p. 44).

A meta-analysis study by Sowell (1989) indicated that long-term instruction using concrete materials increase mathematical learning. The study also indicated that when teachers know how to use concrete materials, the positive attitude of students toward mathematics increases. The concept of "teachers who know how to use concrete materials" is important, and we will examine it later on in this chapter.

The Hobby Industry Association (2002) requested that an independent educational research organization study the impact of using hands-on craft projects in the core curriculum. A total of 76 teachers and more than 1,600 K-6 students participated in the study, which consisted of teacher surveys, student surveys, and student knowledge application tasks. The tasks asked students to use writing and drawing to apply their knowledge of what they had been studying to new situations. The results were clear:

1. Students who were in classes that used hand-on projects about 50% of their time scored an average of 83 out of a possible 100. This score compared with an average score of 75 for students who spent about 12% of their time on hands-on projects.
2. Ninety percent of the teachers indicated that hands-on projects help students understand basic ideas better.
3. Eighty-five percent of the teachers agreed that long-term hands-on projects enable students to understand in greater depth.

11.2.1   The Kinesthetic Mode and Elementary/Middle School Students

Druyan (1997) examined three studies involving the use of kinesthetic movement in the development of scientific reasoning in children from 5 to 12. The first study focused on an understanding of length, the second compared the effects of four types of conflicts (visual, kinesthetic, and two social) on the understanding of balance, and the third compared the effect of the kinesthetic with the visual. In all three studies, the kinesthetic mode was the most effective in fostering cognitive awareness.

A study by Glenberg et al. (2004) involved three experiments with first- and second-grade children. After reading a short text, the children manipulated models of the objects and characters in the readings. The results of the experiments suggest that manipulation and imagined manipulation enhanced reading performance.

In a study done by Marley, Levin, and Glenberg (2007), 45 Native American students from third through seventh grade who were diagnosed with academic learning difficulties listened to narrative passages. Some children manipulated toy objects representing the story content; other students observed the results of the experimenter manipulating the toys; and a third group of students thought about the content of the stories. Both the manipulative and visual strategies statistically outperformed the condition in which students thought about the story.

11.2.2   The Kinesthetic Mode and Secondary Students

Manipulatives have been shown to be effective for secondary students. Aburime (2007) examined an experiment done in Nigeria on the effectiveness of simple geometric manipulatives on the understanding of students. The results of this study indicated that students who were taught with manipulatives outperformed other students.

Snyder (2000) examined the relationship between student academic achievement and learning styles and multiple intelligences. The study indicated that the majority of these high-school students were tactile/kinesthetic learners.

Park (1997) examined the learning styles of Korean, Mexican, and Armenian-American secondary students; the results were then compared with those of Anglo students. In this study, 10 high schools in the Los Angeles and southern California participated. All of these schools had ESL classes, as well as a diverse student population. All four ethnic groups demonstrated a preference for a kinesthetic learning style, and all four showed a minor preference for a tactile learning style. What is the implication for the

Constructivist teacher? It is that the kinesthetic mode does not distinguish ethnicity, at least on the secondary-school level.

11.2.3 The Kinesthetic Mode and Special-Needs Students

Cass et al. (2003) studied the effects of manipulatives on the learning and problem-solving ability of middle-school and high-school students who were diagnosed with LD in mathematics. The study used modeling, prompting, guided practice, independent practice, and manipulative training to study two topics: perimeter and area problem-solving. The results showed that not only did the students acquire problem-solving skills but they also maintained these skills over a two-month period and transferred these skills to a format that used paper and pencil.

Kraemer (1996) reported on a study in which 300 Hispanic students taking developmental English classes at different levels were surveyed to determine their preferred learning style. While the results indicated that the students did not like group work, they did prefer an auditory and tactile learning method.

Manual communication has been shown to aid students who have been diagnosed as having severe reading disabilities. Blackburn, Bonvillian, and Ashby (1984) discussed the case of two adolescent boys who were reading disabled. Over a five-month period, these two students were trained in finger spelling and sign language. The two boys demonstrated improvement; the report attributed some of the improvement to the kinesthetic training.

Modeling clay and cardboard can be used to create inexpensive devices that can be used to help visually challenged students learn statistics. Gibson and Darron (1999) described how devices such as the normal curve and regression lines made of clay helped a blind student learn statistics. This method also included the use of bar graphs made from cardboard that depicted results from different groups. By using these concrete tools, the student mastered the content and passed each of the four examinations.

But it is not just the learning disabled or physically challenged who benefit from the kinesthetic mode. Rayneri, Gerber, and Wiley (2006) examined the learning styles of 80 gifted students in grades 6, 7, and 8. The results indicated that in the content areas of social studies and science there is a correlation between higher grade point averages and persistence and motivation—not surprising—and the auditory, tactile, and kinesthetic modes.

11.2.4 Other Demographics

It is well established that today's male student is not reading or writing as well as his female counterpart. King and Gurian (2006) discussed a study in which "boy-friendly" strategies—including spatial-kinesthetic learning—were used in the classroom. On the stat test, boys showed substantial gains.

11.3   Some Caveats about Manipulatives

Despite the positive findings, some evidence indicates that manipulatives may not empower students to learn more. McNeil and Jarvin (2007) examined the research on manipulatives and found both positive and negative effects from the use of manipulatives. They discuss studies indicating that students who could use manipulatives to *demonstrate* their understanding had a difficult time using that knowledge to solve *written* problems. McNeil and Jarvin discussed a study in which some students were taught a procedure for solving double-digit subtraction use manipulatives, and other students were taught by a written method. Posttest results indicated that the students using manipulatives did worse than the other students. McNeil and Jarvin presented two possible reasons for this result. First, manipulatives may lead students to focus on having fun. Second, manipulatives may require students to use dual representation; that is, the manipulative is thought of as an object itself and as also as a conceptual symbol. Viadero (2007) similarly concluded that students may not capable of connecting the manipulative with the concept they are studying.

For the Constructivist teacher, there is a clear message here: Students do not necessarily *connect between the concept and the manipulative.* The Constructivist teacher, in using manipulatives, must set up an environment in which the students can create their own connection between the manipulative and the concept being taught. Simply telling them the connection will not achieve the desired result.

Viadero's examination of studies on manipulatives brought some light to the challenge. She discussed a study in which students were taught geometry in three ways: using a Logo computer program, using manipulatives in combination with paper and pencil, and using the textbook only. On a test given after instruction, the Logo group and the manipulative group outperformed the textbook group. However, on a test given three weeks later, the Logo group outperformed the other two groups. One explanation given was that working with a computer enables students to be more explicit about their learning; instead of mindlessly manipulate objects, the students had to type in commands that required them to quantify directions by providing the exact degree or exact length of a side.

11.4   The Kinesthetic Mode and Constructivist Teaching

How can the Constructivist teacher best structure the classroom environment so that the students can connect the kinesthetic activities and manipulatives with the concept to be learned? Raphael and Wahlstrom (1989) stressed the *importance of the role of the teacher* in the use of manipulatives. In a study of the use of manipulatives by Ontario Grade 8 mathematics teachers, they found that *occasional use* of instructional aids in conjunction with course coverage resulted in higher student achievement in both plane figures and informal transformations. Raphael and Strom further noted that "more experienced teachers may have more valid grounds for their selection of aids than less experienced teachers" (p. 189). One could also hypothesize that more experienced teachers know how to better connect the learning aids to the concept being taught.

Let's take another look at the example from the beginning of the chapter. The kinesthetic activity is part of solving an authentic situation (airplane speed and wind direction). The class is involved in typical Constructivist activities: cooperative learning, discussions, comparison with other groups, and alternative problem-solving methods. And the teacher is constantly connecting the kinesthetic situation (paper and ruler manipulation) to the concept to be learned (equation solving). Thus, the students are aware as they manipulate objects that the aim of the lesson is to create a generalization or rule.

Manipulatives and kinesthetic activities can play other roles. The previously mentioned research by Druyan points to the effectiveness of kinesthetic disequilibrium; manipulatives can be used to "Rattle their cages"—to create cognitive disequilibrium.

EXERCISE 11.1:
Creating Kinesthetic Disequilibrium in Basic Aviation

One of the concepts used in aviation is that of a great circle. Since the world is not flat, the shortest distance between two points is what is referred to as a "great circle." For example, Tokyo is south of Chicago, but to fly from Chicago to Tokyo via a great circle (the shortest route) requires the plane to go up into Canada and Alaska, and then down toward Tokyo. The reason is that the globe is not a perfect sphere. Thus, the world gets less wide as one moves away from the equator. In this case the world is less wide up in Canada and Alaska, and this is why the great circle route goes up toward the less wide part of the world first, and then down toward Tokyo. While the determination of the distance a plane flies via the Great Circle route requires trigonometry, this activity enables students to create an understanding of the concept of a great circle; this activity acts as a "lead in" to the trigonometric application. When students truly understand the nature of a great circle, they can then construct trigonometric methods for finding this distance. This activity uses a Constructivist/kinesthetic approach to presenting this concept.

1. Have students get into groups of two.
2. Give each group of students a globe and a long piece of string.

Have each group place one end of the string at Chicago and the other at Tokyo (see pictures below) and pull the string as tight as possible. Remind them that the shortest distance between two points is a straight line (represented by the piece of string).

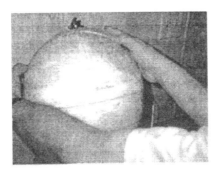

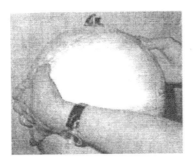

Figure 11.11

3. Ask the students what the shortest distance between two points is, and then have them describe the path of the string. Why is this

happening? Through pair/shares and three-step interviews, have students create statements and conclusions such as the following:

a. On the surface of the globe, the shortest distance between two points is an arc that goes up to the more narrow part of the globe.

b. On the surface of the globe, straight lines are replaced by arcs.

c. On the surface of the globe, distances depend on how far the arc is from the equator.

This exercise then leads to a more detailed discussion on great circles and their relation to trigonometry.

Notes: A variation is the "Chicago to Rome Problem." While it seems strange, Rome basically lies due east of Chicago (Rome has latitude of 41 degrees 54 minutes, and Chicago has latitude of 41 degrees and 50 minutes). As before, have the students hold the string as tight as possible and place one end at Chicago and the other at Rome. Measure that length with a ruler. Then add tick marks along the 41 degrees 50 minute latitude line and place a string along it. Find the length of the string and compare the two lengths. The length of the string representing the due east direction will be longer; again, use cooperative groups to discuss this observation.

EXERCISE 11.2:
Creating Kinesthetic Disequilibrium with Division of Fractions

Most of us grew up with the notion that "division means to make smaller." However, we have all gotten our "cages rattled" when we divide a whole number by a fraction, say, $12 \div 1/2 = 24$, and find that the answer is larger than numbers in the original problem.

This activity is part of a larger unit on dividing by fractions; the lesson objectives include understanding that division does not always mean to "make smaller" and mastering the procedures for determining the quotient when dividing by a number in fractional form.

1. Using masking tape, lay out a number line using a length smaller those of a student's stride as the unit of measure.

2. Have students to take two strides at a time, and ask them how many times it will take to get them to the end. (Repeat with three strides and so on.)

$$12 \div 2 = 6 \qquad 12 \div 3 = 4 \qquad 12 \div 4 = 3$$

3. Now ask: What if you take half a stride? One-third a stride? Actually have the students do this.

4. On the board should be number statements such as:

$$12 \div 1/2 = 24 \qquad 12 \div 1/3 = 36$$

5. Now ask the following: Before, our quotient had numbers smaller than 12; now the quotient has numbers larger than 12. Why?

6. Have each student write a paragraph explaining that division does not always make smaller.

Notes: A kinesthetic activity is designed to "rattle their cage"; students now have constructed the situation where there is cognitive disequilibrium. It is important to have students fill out and put a chart for this on the board, so they can keep track of the pattern. The writing activity is important because it enables the student to construct the words to describe their understanding of the kinesthetic activity; this is an example of "turning the kaleidoscope" because it provides the opportunity to connect different modes.

EXERCISE 11.3:
Using Kinesthetic Activities to Develop Phonemic Awareness
in Kindergarten Students

This activity is used to help students learn how to blend syllables to create a word. The teacher has the students sit in front of her and has the students follow her lead.

1. In this example, the teacher wants the students to blend syllables to form the word "cupcake."

2. As the teacher pushes her hand forward, she says "cup"; the students then copy this behavior.

3. The teacher pushes the other hand forward and says "cake." The students copy this behavior.

4. The teacher then joins the two hands together and says "cupcake." The class also models this action.

5. The teacher then holds up a candlestick. If the students don't know what it is, the teacher can recite the short poem "Jack be nimble, Jack be quick, Jack jump over the candlestick" and have the students get up and jump over it. Then the students try to explain what two elements are combined to make up this word.

Notes: The students can be invited to think of other words like this. This will have them be "Captain of their own ship." Some possibilities are bookend, bedspread, and skateboard.

EXERCISE 11.4:
Using Kinesthetic Activities to Create New Understanding in Reading Comprehension

This activity is an extension of the activity described in the study by Marley et al. (2007), in which students are read a story and then use toys to act out the story. It is intended for young readers.

The students are asked to reconsider rewriting the ending. Students can act out the change using the toys and rehearse different options readily with the toys. As they do this, they can verbalize their reasoning. For example, consider *Goldilocks and the Three Bears*. The teacher should get three toy bears of different sizes, a female doll to represent Goldilocks, three toy chairs of different sizes, and three toy plates. After the students use the toys to act out the story, they can create other endings to act out (One bear leaves, Goldilocks becomes friends with the bears, etc.).

11.5   Drama and Constructivism

Drama is a vehicle that can naturally get students to connect school to their personal lives. While content areas like history may seem unconnected to the personal experiences of students, Kornfeld and Leyden (2005) saw the impact of drama:

> By acting out those stories, students can get intensely involved in history—disturbed, excited, and committed to learning more about the subject—while seeing how their lives in the present are connected to issues and concerns of the past. (p. 230)

The assertion that drama enables students to connect history to their personal lives points to the possible Constructivist nature of drama—making connections and embedding an experience in other experiences. But how can this be done? One possibility is through role playing. Comer (2005) described the effectiveness of role playing in a critical care nursing course. A scenario was given to students, with one student assuming the role of a patient, and four others take on nursing roles. The rest of the class members served as a resource element. The results showed a marked decline in the number of students failing the first exam. Similarly, Zehr (2004) examined role playing in a History of Psychology class. In one exercise students played the role of members of a psychology department that was deciding to hire William James for a position. In another exercise students were given names of prominent historical figures in psychology and were given time to write a short summary about that person. In the speed-dating fashion, the students then paired off with a partner and exchanged information. This continued until everyone had spoken to one another. Students then wrote what historical figure (other than their own) had the most influence on applied psychology; students also had to defend their position. Student evaluation of these activities indicated that they believed that this type of role playing was very effective.

While many resources are available to help teachers use drama and role playing in their content areas, here are a few activities that present a "Constructivist" twist.

EXERCISE 11.5:
Using Drama to "Rattle Their Cages" in a History Class—"Just the Facts"

Have students get in groups, and assign each group to a topic that the class just studied, such as the Boston Tea Party or the Crossing of the Potomac. Each group is to perform a skit about the topic, but they are to misrepresent a fact or person or so forth. The rest of the class members are to work together with their partner to find the misrepresentation.

Notes: An activity such as this can be used in place of the traditional "review for the test" activity.

EXERCISE 11.6:
Using Drama to "Rattle Their Cages" in a History Class— Time Warp

Stage a debate between presidential candidates for an upcoming election, using presidential contenders or well-known figures from that era. For example, use Woodrow Wilson and FDR, or Coolidge and John Davis.

Students must be given a list of questions beforehand so they can prepare their answers; they must write a paper on this, discussing how they predict what that person's response would be. This must be backed up by what was said in the text, other resources, and class activities. The process of backing up their predictions is an essential element of this assignment.

Notes: To engage the entire class in the Constructivist process, one could instead have a town hall type of debate, in which the questions are submitted by the audience (from a list of prepared questions, probably). After each candidate has answered the question, someone from the audience could ask a follow-up question to one or the other of the candidates, with the aim of pinpointing discrepancies in the answer or making the one candidate compare his views with the other candidate's. Also, have students from the "studio audience" write a letter to the editor (250 words or less) on who won the debate and why.

EXERCISE 11.7:
Using Drama to "Turn the Kaleidoscope"—Finish the Story

Suppose that you are studying the Battle of Gettysburg. Have students portray the different sides of a court martial for General Lee or Jeb Stuart or some other general involved in the battle. One student will be the accused, one the officer who presents the case, one an officer/lawyer who defends the accused, and five students the jury (a panel of officers).

Notes: To engage the entire class in the Constructivist process, everyone will have to contribute to the research before the court martial. Have the students work in pairs, each pair preparing a list of 2 charges and their seriousness, as well as a possible defense. Then collect the charges and merge them to create a final list. Give the justification for each charge to the lawyer presenting the case. Give the defense to the defense lawyer.

EXERCISE 11.8:
Using Podcasting to Create a Constructivist Environment

Here is an activity that blends technology with drama.

Have students get in groups to produce a podcast that creates an audio commercial about a topic they have studied. Students are to be put in groups and then are to be assigned or choose a topic that they are to create a short podcast about.

Students producing the podcast would have to write a reflection; one possible prompt would be to have students discuss the challenges of producing an audio product versus producing a product people can see.

Students listening to the podcast would be required to write a reflection; a possible prompt would be how listening to this would be different from seeing a dramatization.

Notes: This can be modified to a "radio commercial" that is recorded with a recorder. Another variation would be to use this as part of an end of the semester or year review.

12

A Metastrategy for Note Taking

How many times have you heard the following statement: "I usually don't take notes; if I do, I always miss something the teacher is saying"? Or, how often, at the end of a lecture, have you asked a student about a point he had written, only to find he could not understand what was meant by the words he'd hastily scribbled on paper? These challenges are faced by teachers every day. But a close examination of note taking and applying Constructivist principles to it will result in a class environment in which students are autonomous and are creating their own knowledge through note taking.

12.1 Research on Note Taking versus No Note Taking

To take notes or not to take notes? That is the initial question all Constructivist teachers must answer. Researchers have examined that question and provide some insights.

Kobayashi (2006) conducted a meta-analysis of 33 studies. The purpose of this analysis was to look at how much the combination of taking and

The Comprehensive Handbook of Constructivist Teaching, pages 147–155
Copyright © 2010 by Information Age Publishing
147

reviewing notes enhance student learning. Kobayashi concluded that the combination did offer considerable benefit.

Einstein, Morris, and Smith (1985) reported on two experiments that looked at the encoding function of note taking and the processing differences between successful and less successful students who attended lectures. The first experiment involved two sets of students: one consisted of students who took notes, and the other consisted of students who listened during a lecture. The results indicated that the note takers recalled a higher number of high-importance propositions than low-importance propositions, while non-note takers recalled an equal amount of low-importance propositions as high-importance propositions. *Note taking empowers students to organize information more effectively.*

Similar results were found in a study by Kiewra et al. (1988) in which college students viewed a 19-minute videotaped lecture. A week later the students were provided with three different forms of notes (a complete text, a linear outline, or a matrix form), with a fourth group acting as a control group that did not receive notes. Results from three performance tests indicated that the control group scored the lowest.

12.2 Note Taking and Learning

Let's take a look at possible explanations for the positive effects of note taking.

12.2.1 Structuring Notes

The Einstein et al. (1985) study compared successful note takers and nonsuccessful note takers. An analysis of the notes taken indicated that both groups appeared to organize and structure the information, and both groups noted more high-importance information than low-importance information. The two groups differed, however, in the degree to which they organized their notes. The differences in recall between the two groups point to the fact that "recall differences between successful and less successful students were due to factors occurring at encoding (rather than at retrieval) and to factors involved more with what ideas were included in the notes than with note-taking style" (p. 531). The study results indicated that "successful students have more powerful organizational skills for structuring expository materials" (p. 531). The phrases "factors occurring at encoding" and "structuring expository materials" imply that the key point of note taking is that of restructuring and making personal meaning of notes and this implies our Constructivist strategy of "Turning the kaleidoscope."

In a study done by Palkovitz and Lore (1980) that examined note taking and note review, the results indicated that students get answers incorrect not because their lecture notes are either incorrect or incomplete but because they do not review and learn the material adequately. Not learning the material adequately implies that the students are not making connections between their notes and their previous knowledge. This implies that the Constructivist strategy of "Turn the kaleidoscope" might be needed. Gettinger and Seibert (2002) extended this idea; in discussing successful study skills they examined the effectiveness of summarization and stated that for a summary to be generative, "the learner's own words and experiences are used to construct novel sentences that make connections between concepts and relate new information to prior knowledge" (p. 8).

- ▪ These studies imply that effective note taking must follow a Constructivist approach in which *the learner restructures, rewords, and connects to previous knowledge,* in order to make the lecture notes his own property.

The question then is "What are the nuts and bolts of doing so?" The use of "kaleidoscope" strategies will help; but another aspect also must be explored, and that is the aspect of what a lecture environment that does this looks like. The following paragraphs address this question.

12.2.2   *The Best Way of Note Taking*

Is there a "best" way of note taking? A study by Kiewra et al. (1988) compared three note-taking formats: their conventional format for taking notes, an outline arrangement, and a matrix arrangement. The outline and matrix formats, according to this study, enabled students to foster internal connections by making superordinate-subordinate relations *within topics* transparent. Since categories and subcategories are provided, all notes that are transcribed are connected to another idea, thus starting the process of forming a network of connections. The matrix format also has the advantage of building connections *across topics.*

Consequently, the authors expected that matrix note taking, complemented by essay writing, would be the most effective learning strategy: the matrix note-taking format because it fostered two-dimensionality and the essay because it provided the opportunity to synthesize topics. However, the outline format proved to be superior. The reason? The outline format contained more ideas than did the other two formats. In particular, a matrix format limits note-taking cues. A flexible outline that coincides with the lecture's changing structure is more effective than that of a matrix.

The study did indicate, however, that a matrix arrangement with cues or subtopics along the side margin would be comparable to a flexible outline. The study also stated that combining the outline format with essay writing maximizes delayed recall.

The study by Kiewra et al. similarly examined three types of note taking—a complete text of the notes, a linear outline, and a matrix—as well as no notes. The outline and matrix forms both resulted in higher recall than did the text notes. However, only the matrix form resulted in higher *transfer.*

12.2.3 Partial Notes versus Full Notes

Another parameter for note taking is that of partial notes vs. provided full notes. Kierwa (1985) examined two types of instructor notes given to students before the lecture: full notes, containing all of the main ideas and details, and skeletal notes, highlighting the main points. Based on several studies, Kierwa concluded that partial outlines usually leads to higher achievement than does standard note taking.

Annis (1981) examined the situation in which college students took either their own notes or used full or partial notes given to students while they were listening to a lecture. All students participated in all three treatments on a rotating basis. The results provide evidence that the format of the notes students use does influence on achievement. For both the multiple-choice and essay tests, students using the full notes format did not score as well as students using their own or the partial notes format.

Kayatama and Crooks (2003) investigated the effectiveness of complete vs. partial electronic notes. The results indicated that, while there did not appear to be any advantage to partial notes when it came to learning factual information, partial notes did seem aid in applying concepts to novel situations and for recalling text structure.

The effects of provided notes and personal notes were studied by Morrison, McLaughlin, and Rucker (2002). In this study most first-year medical students heavily annotated the set of provided notes given to them, indicating that students do process the semantic contents by taking notes. Also, students indicated that they spend 25% of their study time on their own notes, which compares with the 30% of study time spent reviewing the instructor provided notes.

12.2.4 Interactive Engagement

Hake studied the effects of interactive-engagement (IE) on students. He defined this as methods designed to help develop conceptual learning through a hands-on and a minds-on approach; this approach included immediate feedback through discussion with teachers and peers. This study compared the effects of the IE format for a class vs. "traditional" procedures. He found that IE strategies increase problem-solving ability.

- The concept of *interactive engagement* provides cues for the Constructivist teacher to consider for developing lecture activities.

12.3   Note Taking and Constructivism

The discussion from the previous section indicates that there are some principles that the Constructivist teacher can follow when considering note taking activities in the classroom. These are summarized below:

1. It is not just taking notes that enables a student to learn; rather it is an *active encoding process* that enables learning.
2. During note taking, the students must *use their own words and experiences.*
3. A *flexible outline form* of lecture notes provides the logistics for creating more ideas.
4. *Partial notes* empower the students to view the thought process of the teacher but to also encode using their own notes.

12.4   Interactive Lecture

I have effectively and enthusiastically used an instrument called "The Interactive Lecture" (IL) that applies the above principles. The IL is actually a metastrategy and platform that enable the instructor to present Constructivist activities in a lecture environment. It is an outline of instructor ideas of the topic to be studied that contains topic headings, activities, and space for the students to create their own ideas. It is passed out to students before the introduction of the topic.

The following is an example of an interactive lecture that comes from my class in Measurement and Evaluation. The topic of the interactive lecture is performance/authentic/alternative assessment. It is part of a larger assignment that places the student in the role of a first-year teacher who must prepare an assessment plan with PowerPoint slides to be presented to parents at an open house (this larger assignment is an example of problem-based learning, which will be discussed in the next chapter). This outline is passed out to students at the beginning of class. While there is space for students to write in, this example will use the space to provide commentary.

Performance-Based Assessment
Dr. Pelech

Name _____

1. **The Big Question**: Your principal calls you into his office and says, *"I heard you are doing a lot of this 'performance-based assessment stuff'; I don't see how this will help with our test scores. I want you to stop doing this and get the kids ready for those state tests."*

   In the space below, write a few lines describing what you would say to your principal.

   [Students are given the opportunity to be "Captain of Their Ship" by creating an original response to an authentic situation (TV Reality Show), and they are encoding the concept of "performance-based assessment" by connecting it to their own philosophy.]

2. **Pair/Share**

   [Students participate in a pair/share to explain how they responded to the opening prompt. Here students are given the opportunity to do more active encoding by "Turning the kaleidoscope" and "rattling their cage." They are to put their ideas in the space provided.]

3. **Partner/Group Share**

   [The process of "Rattling their cages" and "Turning the kaleidoscope" is continued by having students put on the board what they have learned from their partner.]

4. **Summarizing the Sharing Activity.** Where do we go from here?

   [To gauge student understanding, the instructor leads an informal discussion on what the students still feel they need to know to apply the concept to their own practice. Again, students put their notes in the provided space.]

5. **Three Terms.** The terms "authentic assessment," "performance assessment," and "alternative assessment" are often used interchangeably. While they are closely related, there are some slight distinctions. Using what you already know about these three

terms, complete the diagram below. Do this without the use of your book. Please do this with your partner.

[There is a slight distinction between these terms, and this activity is used to activate student prior knowledge by putting it in the visual form (another example of active encoding and "Turning the kaleidoscope"). While this example provides a graphical organizer, students may already have knowledge in designing and completing one, so providing them with one may not be needed.]

6. **Class Share**

   [Here student volunteers share their organizers with the rest of the class and explain their reasoning. The instructor moderates a class discussion on any differences and then compares this to how the book defines these terms (Rock their boat; Turn the kaleidoscope, Captain of their own ship). Students sketch out organizers that are different from what they have.]

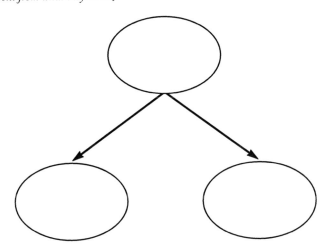

Figure 12.1

7A. **Types of Performance Assessment**

   The instructor puts the following list on the overhead or writes it out on the board:

   ▪ Type a letter of recommendation for a friend that must be no longer than one page.
   ▪ Read an assigned poem out loud in class.
   ▪ Write an essay explaining why the Allies won World War II.
   ▪ Repair an engine in a shop class.

- Write an essay that explains three U.S. military mistakes in Vietnam.
- Create a PowerPoint presentation consisting of five slides that discusses your philosophy of homework.
- Create a PowerPoint presentation that discusses your philosophy of assessment and your grading policy.
- Write a short story.
- Write a short story consisting of 10,000 words that uses two writing techniques discussed in class.

[The instructor tells students to work with their partner to put the list into two groups (in provided space). After this is done, students get with another two-partner group to come to a consensus, and to also come to a consensus concerning the parameters for forming the two groups. This activity is designed to empower students to create a definition of "restricted-response" performance assessments and "extended-response" performance assessments. These are examples of either "restricted response" or "extended response." By having students create two categories, the instructor is tapping into the students' prior knowledge concerning the two terms. Now, the teacher can use cooperative learning and Constructivist questioning techniques by having students explain their reasoning, and then use these responses to construct the respected definitions.]

7B. **Look at the book's examples and definitions. Let's discuss how the book's definitions compare to what this class has created.**

[Here the instructor uses cooperative learning and class discussion to compare the book's definitions to what the class has created. This can be done through class discussion, blackboard presentations, and so forth. This activity is Constructivist because it "Rocks their boat" and "Turns their kaleidoscope." The students now have created a definition of these terms by creating a network of concepts between what the book says and what different members of the class have said.]

7C. **Examples of restricted-response assessments and extended-response assessments from your practice.**

[The teacher gives students time to develop at least two examples of each category from the grade/level they plan to teach. Then they are grouped by the instructor by category (elementary, middle school, and high school). Students in each of the groups share with others their examples. The students put on the board their examples and the examples of their partners.]

8. **Wild Card**

[Here the instructor uses cooperative learning and class discussion to discuss what the next category of the lesson should be. This may consist of topics they want to learn

more about or a review of topics that must be cleared up. This activity is open-ended and surprisingly effective, especially when students are encouraged to present their own ideas.]

9. **Closing Activity**

["The Tollbooth" problem has been an effective closing activity. Just as drivers must stop and "pay toll" on the toll way, students must "pay toll" in order to leave class. The students take out a half-sheet of paper and write a response to the following prompts (usually a few lines that will take no more than three to five minutes). Here are a few possible prompts.]

- Discuss how you will now answer the "Big Question."
- Discuss what you learned today that surprised you.
- Discuss what you learned from your partner that represents a real change from the way you have been thinking.
- Discuss whether you believe that performance assessment will enable students to think at a higher level than traditional paper-and-pencil tests. Be sure to explain your reasoning.

13

Delivering Constructivism through Problem-Based Learning

I spent more than twenty years in the Army Reserves as an officer, and in 1996 I was activated for a period of approximately eight months; within a few short weeks I went from being a high-school math teacher to an army staff officer. During my "free time" I did much reflecting on this experience, and I came to the following personal revelation. As a transportation staff officer I made many decisions, but they were not decisions that were presented as a "clean," well-defined problem (like the math problems in a textbook). In real life your boss does not hand you a well-defined problem for which you can easily and directly apply an already established algorithm. In real life you are handed (usually at 4:00 on a Friday before a vacation) a messy, confusing, loosely defined situation, for which you must define the problem and must structure the thinking processes in order to create the best possible solution (unlike a clear-cut right answer as is presented in academic situations). Messy, ill-defined problems were characteristic of my life as an army officer. In the real world, successful people must use higher order-thinking skills and established algorithms in order to take a messy

The Comprehensive Handbook of Constructivist Teaching, pages 157–168
Copyright © 2010 by Information Age Publishing
All rights of reproduction in any form reserved.

situation and define the problem, construct questions to be answered in order to solve the problem, rank these questions define the resources to be used, construct possible solutions, debrief the problem, and then start this cycle over again.

When I returned to civilian life, I not only tried to do more applications of the math I was teaching, but I also started to study Constructivism in earnest. I tried to combine Constructivism with practical applications. Unfortunately, my implementation of this philosophy was centered on understanding a predetermined, well-defined principle and then applying it to a predetermined, clearly stated problem. This scenario did not empower the students to develop the higher-order thinking skills of defining problems and creating solutions for a messy situation. When I read about problem-based learning (PBL), I felt that I had found the instrument for translating my Constructivist philosophy into a pedagogy that would result in students demonstrating authentic problem-solving skills.

13.1   What Is Problem-Based Learning?

PBL is pedagogy and a curricular organizer that use a hands-on, minds-on, experiential approach. As with Constructivism, PBL has many versions and many educators who claim to implement it. Nevertheless, several features are constant with all versions of PBL:

1. An authentic, ill-defined problem starts the instruction, and the solution of this problem is the focus of classroom activities (as opposed to learning isolated algorithms and concepts).
2. The authentic problem is presented to the student in the form it would be presented in the "real world."
3. Students are given personal ownership of their learning; as in many real-life situations, there is no set solution; thus, students must create their own "right solution."
4. Solutions to problems will cross content or domain lines.
5. Learning occurs in small groups.
6. Teachers act as guides, asking questions instead of providing right/wrong responses.
7. Resources for solving the problem run the gamut of what is found in the "real world": books, journals, experts in the filed, newspapers, and so forth.
8. New knowledge is created through group discussion, self-reflection, and comparison with other group members, questioning

other group members, and a continual assessment of the developing solution.

We've already seen some of these elements in earlier chapters. One example was from a college algebra class in which students were to find equations of straight lines and to solve linear equations. Embedding these content topics into a PBL context resulted in a scenario in which students work as reporters for a new sports magazine that is lacking in female readership. The editor wants the reporter to write an article titled "Will Women Outperform Men in Athletics?" In this situation students will have to plot times for female and male athletes in the 100-meter dash and use algebra to help them create the article.

Another example from a college algebra class is that of students taking on the role of a consultant to the governor of a specific state; the students must write a letter indicating that the current system of assigning numbers and letters to license plates will not be effective in the coming years, since the state will run out of options. Here students must use the content knowledge of permutations, combinations, and exponential functions to address this problem. Students do not learn about permutations and combinations in isolation. Rather, they connect these ideas to the solution of a real-world problem.

Other possible authentic problems include determining what to do with computer hardware that is thrown out, or deciding where to locate a new airport, or developing a system that replaces the Electoral College, or analyzing whether a shipping company should change its entire fleet to use alternative fuels. All of these problems are authentic and ill-defined; that is, they can be solved in many different ways.

13.2   PBL Model

In many of the models of PBL, the ill-defined situation can be solved through many different domains. For many elementary, middle, and secondary teachers this may be a disadvantage because of the requirements of mandated state-testing. Today's practitioner is obligated to cover certain content, and the large degree of open-endedness presented by PBL could result in certain content not being covered in the required depth. One way to address this situation is by designing problems that, while open-ended, still require the application of content skills for a solution. Clearly defining the content standard and skills first, and then designing an authentic and open-ended solution around these, is an effective way to bring Constructivism and PBL to the students and still meet state requirements. We'll discuss more of this later in this chapter.

How do teachers find or create ill-defined problems? A good starting point is to use the textbook. Many math textbooks have practical applications at the end of the unit or chapter. Also, publications such as *USA Today, the Wall Street Journal, People Magazine, Road and Track Magazine,* and *Sports Illustrated* offer good examples. Another approach to finding a source of ill-defined problems is to consult with individuals who work in the field. Pilots, policemen, and architects are rich sources of applications for math classes. For applications in education courses, the author has found principals and teachers are helpful.

Some models of PBL include those in which students work in small groups with an instructor, independently gather information, report back to their groups, and discuss information with group members. This method has been effective with mature learners, but it may not be effective for all learners in the settings that many teachers find themselves. One solution is to use an interactive lecture and rough drafts to structure the "define and redefine the central issue" and "create possible solutions" phases. The interactive lecture, while providing a Constructivist environment, allows for teacher guidance and modeling. Figure 13.1 represents the PBL process that I have implemented and used successfully. This model is a modification of the model used by the Illinois Mathematics and Science Academy.

13.3 PBL and Research

It is important that Constructivist teachers base their practice on research, and this principle must also apply to PBL. Over the years researchers have sought to evaluate the effectiveness of PBL. Let's look at some of this research.

A meta-analysis review of English-language international literature from 1972 to 1992 indicated the effectiveness of PBL for medical students (Albanese & Mitchell, 1993). The results showed that medical students trained by PBL do as well as or better than students trained by traditional methods in faculty evaluations and on clinical examinations. In a similar study of medical students Vernon and Blake (1993) conducted five separate meta-analyses on 35 studies representing 19 institutions from 1970 through 1992. This study looked at student opinions and attitudes toward their respective programs and found PBL to be significantly more effective than other methods. Still another systematic review was made of the effects of PBL on medical students after they had graduated (Koh et al., 2008). The results from this study showed that PBL during medical school had positive effects on physicians after graduation; these positive effects were in social and cognitive dimensions.

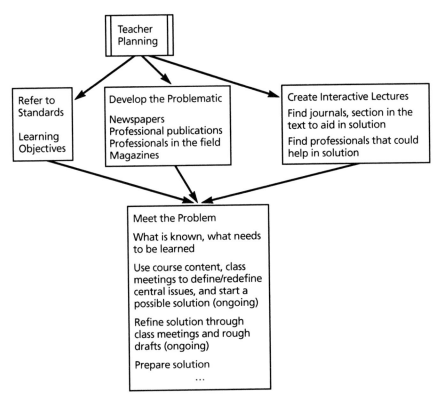

Figure 13.1

And no, it is not only medical students who benefit from PBL. In a year-long community college leadership course, participants indicated their support for PBL (Herron & Major, 2004), stating that PBL was an effective method for developing leadership, collaborative skills, and research.

PBL has also been effective at the middle-school and high-school levels. Gordon et al. (2001) looked at the effect of PBL on urban minority middle-school students. While the classrooms allowed for PBL activities only 2% of the time, results showed that PBL resulted in increased science learning. Gallagher, Stepien, and Rosenthal (1992) conducted a study that compared high-school students taught by PBL with students taught by another method. The purpose of the study was to determine the effects of PBL on the spontaneous use of problem-solving steps. The results showed significant changes for the PBL group that were not observed in the other group. One important effect was that the experimental group was stronger in "problem-finding"; this is the step in which students articulate the central issue to the ill-defined problem. More recently, Sungur and Tekkaya (2006) examined the effects of PBL on tenth-grade biology students. Their study showed that PBL students had higher levels of intrinsic goal orientation, task value, critical thinking, and self-regulation.

13.4 Examples of PBL

This section presents three examples of PBL in the classroom.

13.4.1 Example 1

Our first example comes from a college Measurement and Evaluation class.

1. Teacher Planning

The objectives for the first couple of chapters were to list and know the purposes of assessment, to list and know the different types of assessment, and to know how to use assessment to plan for instruction. To translate these into a PBL/Constructivist assignment, I had a conversation with a local elementary principal. This principal stated that, for the first few weeks of school, teachers should have an assessment plan that includes the following:

- A philosophy of assessment.
- The different types of assessment.
- The purposes of assessment.
- The types of informal assessments used.
- The grading scale used.
- The role of homework in assessment and grading.

He also indicated that teachers should also have a clear understanding of the assessment questions used by state assessments. Moreover, teachers should prepare a PowerPoint presentation outlining the assessment plan to be used at Open House.

2. Meet the Problem

For this phase of the problem, the instructor moderated a conference call in which the principal actually discussed with the class what he would expect new teachers to know and do about assessment in the first couple of weeks of school. During this conference call students would take notes and would ask questions of the principal.

The instructor then passed out the following handout.

Scenario

This scenario is based on the conference call that we had. As a new teacher you are to write an assessment plan based on the conference call. The plan that you write will be an artifact that you can bring to an interview to show a prospective principal that you have a solid plan.

3. Identify What You Know and What You Need to Learn

The instructor then works with the class to fill in the chart; typical responses for this scenario are shown below:

Know

- Need an assessment plan that identifies your philosophy, purpose of assessment, types, grade scales, role of homework.
- Need PowerPoint slides.

Need to Learn

- What are the purposes of an assessment?
- What are the types of assessment?
- What is the definition of informal assessment?
- What is formal assessment?
- Should I give homework?
- Is there an official form for a philosophy?
- What goes into a philosophy?
- What should go on slides?
- Any constraints, requirements for slides?

4. Identify the Central Issue

A typical response at this stage is: How can I develop an assessment plan that contains different types of assessment? This central issue is reviewed at the start of every information gathering session (class) so students can have a barometer for gauging how the new information has changed or increased their understanding.

1. Use Course Content and Class Meetings to Develop a Solution.

   The central issue is reviewed, and the following interactive lecture outline is passed out to students. In the examples in this section the spaces that students would use to put their notes in will be used to make editorial comments.

PHILOSOPHY OF ASSESSMENT/EDUCATION
DR. PELECH

Name _____

"The Big Question":

In the era of NCLB, teachers give students tests because ...

[Here prior knowledge is being activated, and the students will begin the process of thinking about the purposes of tests and other assessment. Also, this prompt empowers students to start to connect to the constraints put on classroom assessments through NCLB.]

1. Pair/Share

[Students now put their thoughts into the written mode.]

2. Partner Consensus-Group Share (non-consensus)

[Students must now connect to their partner's thoughts (Turn the Kaleidoscope) by comparing their thoughts with their partner's thoughts. An interesting twist is to put on the board at least one or two ideas that they did not agree on.]

3. Creating a Philosophy of Assessment

What do you plan to assess? Why?

[The purpose of this prompt is to have students begin to create their philosophy of assessment and education. The instructor can cue them on this by encouraging them to connect to the article that they read.]

4. Deciding What an Assessment Would Look Like in Your Classroom. (What would one hear and see if they walked into your classroom?)

[Here students are given the opportunity to synthesize their thoughts and start to put their conceptual thoughts into concrete, observable behaviors.]

5. Group Consensus-Board Share

[Students are put into groups of four and put their consensus ideas on the board (be sure to encourage students that have not yet been to the board to go up to it). Also, people from the group that did not go to the board must explain to the rest of the class what was put on the board.]

6. Categorize—Graphic Organizer

[The instructor leads the class in putting the ideas on the board into a graphical modality.]

7. Purposes of Assessment

[This exercise enables students to connect to the purposes of assessment as defined by the book (Placement, Formative, Diagnostic, and Summative). Most likely, students have not given thought to how they would use placement assessment in the classroom; the instructor can coach them to say they can give a test at the start of the year to see if they are in the correct class, or they can give a test before each unit to see if some students already know the concept, and thus can be given other assignments. The important issue is that the instructor uses the book's ideas to "Turn the kaleidoscope" or "Rattle their Cage."]

8. Central Issue/Possible Solution

[Here students are given the opportunity to redefine the central issue of the scenario and to articulate how what they have learned can help develop a solution.]

There should also be a closing activity to this interactive lecture. Typically, this is a writing activity. For example students can send the instructor an email summarizing what they can use in the scenario.

Next, the teacher can conduct an interactive lecture on performance assessment (this was presented in Chapter 12). Note that not every activity will or should be structured by an interactive lecture. One of the requirements of this scenario is to include homework into the assessment plan. For example, the teacher can pass out four research articles to students in groups of three or four. Students can work in their group to assign an article to each member, who is responsible for reading it and then reporting back to the group. Let's say the articles are labeled A, B, C, and D. When it is time for students to report out, the instructor has all the A's group together, all the B's group together, and so forth. After briefing each other ("Turn the kaleidoscope," "rattle their cage"), students get back to their original group and report what they believe can be used to solve the scenario.

13.4.2   Example 2

Our second example is from a sixth-grade math class that I teach weekly as part of a school-university partnership.

1. Teacher Planning

Three state standards are to be reviewed: multiplying fractions and mixed numbers, solving practical problems that involve whole numbers and fractions, and using instruments to make measurements. What follows is how to convert the requirements from the state standards to a Constructivist/PBL environment.

2. Meet the Problem

After looking at end of book chapters for application problems and after studying the state standards and course objectives, the instructor developed the following scenario.

Student Worksheet Grade Six, December 8–9, 2008
The "Fixit" Scenario

Mrs. Pass has talked Mrs. Spells into "fixing' up her classroom. Mrs. Pass wishes to get a new whiteboard and new tile floor and to buy a special cleaner for all of the desk tops. Mrs. Spells has approved these requests but wants the measurements first. There is, however, a problem: We can't find the rulers, but Mrs. Spells wants the measurements by the end of the day.

3. Identify What You Know and Need to Learn

The teacher works with the class on the "Know, Need to Learn" elements of the problem.

Know	Need To Learn
Mrs. Pass is getting new "stuff"	How can we measure without a ruler?
The new stuff includes a whiteboard, new tile floor, and cleaner for the desktops	Will Mrs. Spells accept guesses?
	What else can we use?
Measurements are due today	How do we allow for mistakes on estimating?

4. Central Focus

A typical response at this stage is: How can we measure everything so we can get it to Mrs. Spells before the end of the day?

5. Gather and Share Information

What follows is a possible interactive lecture that could follow the "Know, Need to Know" part of the lesson.

Name _____

1. Think Pair/Share. Think about what you could do to find the measurements, and write down all of your ideas on the space provided.

   [Some possible responses follow]:

   – Just look at it and guess.

   – Use other things to measure.

[The instructor then steps in and asks students to choose objects that would work. Some possible responses follow.]

– Edge of book

– A pen

– A pencil

– A paper clip

– A stapler

– A key

Now, get with your partner and decide on the top 3 objects to use. Be prepared to justify your answer. Put your answers in the space provided.

2. Class Share. Choose a person to come to the board and write out the top three. Be prepared to discuss your rankings with the class.

   [This exercise gives the teacher the opportunity to see how students are thinking and provides the opportunity for students to discuss any rankings that they do not agree with.]

3. Class Consensus

   [The instructor leads the class in a discussion about which object is easiest to use. If no consensus can be reached, different groups can use different instruments; then different answers can be compared.]

4. The Measurements

   [Let us assume that the students choose a paper clip for the desk top and the edge of the book for the floor. As the students start to measure, the teacher should circulate throughout the room to work with and informally assess the progress of the students. Some students, especially when measuring the whiteboard, will ask if it is OK to "unfold" the paperclip; this is a "teachable" moment in which the teacher can lead a class discussion or use cooperative learning to discuss the advantages and disadvantages of "unfolding" the paper clip.]

5. Stop the Presses—or Not

   [The instructor has miraculously arranged for rulers to show up. This again represents a "teachable" moment because now there can be a class discussion on what to do: stop what you're doing and measure directly with the ruler, continue measuring with the paperclip, or measure how many inches the paper clip (unfolded paper clip) is and multiply that

measurement by how many paper clips it took to measure. With a little encouragement, the class can be led to decide to pursue the last two options.]

6. Finalizing the Measurements

[The students measure the desk and the board by two methods: directly measuring with the ruler, and then measuring with the paperclip and multiplying the number of paperclips by its length in inches. The teacher may want to intervene at this time and make sure that students know how to multiply fractions and mixed numbers. The teacher can then have students compare the results from the different methods and discuss the advantages and disadvantages of each.]

Note: The preceding example represents how PBL can be used in a Constructivist class as a review; this format can also be used to introduce the concept. The teacher could "springboard" off the scenario to teach measuring with a ruler and then the multiplication of mixed numbers; these can then be blended to finish the scenario.

14

Metacognition, Reflection, and Constructivism

Do any of the following sound familiar?

1. I don't know why I performed that step; I just did it.
2. This assignment seems so overwhelming I just don't know where to start.
3. I like how that instructor teaches; I just do not know why. I guess I need to think about it.
4. This assignment does not seem ready to go, but I am not sure what is missing.
5. I do better when I study hard two nights before a test, and then study a little bit the night before.
6. I looked at the rubric, and I still need to finish requirements 3 and 7.
7. I do better when I skim over the material, then go back and read for detail.

The Comprehensive Handbook of Constructivist Teaching, pages 169–173
Copyright © 2010 by Information Age Publishing

8. I read the instructor's comments, but I do not understand the purpose of his last question.
9. If I had to do this assignment over again, I would do things differently.

All of these refer to what is commonly called "metacognition." And what is metacognition? Flavell (1979) called it beliefs about those factors that interact to influence the outcome of cognitive enterprises, namely, person, task, and strategy. Such beliefs are gained from experience and stored in long-term memory. Metacognition can also be thought of as the process of regulating, monitoring, and evaluating cognitions (DiPippa & Peters, 2003). Look at it this way: to create a question is to use cognition, while reflecting on *why you asked the question* is metacognition. Here is another example: to construct a graphic organizer is a cognitive activity, but to *analyze whether this helps you learn* is an example of metacognition.

Thus far, we have examined how one constructs knowledge. In this chapter, we examine a second function of the mind: regulating one's own thinking (thinking about one's thinking). Vygotsky (1962) describes mental self-regulation this way: "We use *consciousness* to denote awareness of the activity of the mind—the consciousness of being conscious" (p. 91). For now, metacognition will be defined as "the conscious process of regulating, monitoring, and developing and monitoring strategies regarding one's thinking."

14.1   Metacognition and Research

Metacognition has been shown to help college students learn. Hall (2001) found that metacognitive skills play an important role in the achievement of these adolescents, and Rezvan, Ahmadi, and Abedi (2006) found that metacongnitive training increased the academic achievement of marginal-scoring Iranian college students. In a study examining college students with learning disabilities, Trainin and Swanson (2005) found that metacognitive performance levels in self-regulation may provide compensation for such students; they attained a GPA as high as did students who were not diagnosed as having a learning disability.

Younger students may also benefit. In a study involving third graders, the effect of metacognitive strategies on reading comprehension was investigated. Results indicated that metacognitive instruction led to the increase in reading comprehension (Bouulware-Gooden et al., 2007). Camahalan (2006) studied the effects of a program that taught metacognitive strategies to four elementary students who were diagnosed with dyslexia. The results suggest that students using metacognitive strategies will benefit.

While metacognitive skills are important for students to learn, it is equally important for teachers to understand how these skills are constructed. Beyer (2008) noted that "skilled thinking rarely develops simply as the result of experience or maturation alone" (p. 224). He noted that proficiency in thinking requires more than indirect teaching. Nietfled, Cao, and Osborne (2005) conducted a study in which undergraduate students practiced metacognitive monitoring throughout an entire semester. Based on the results, the authors believed that "increasing students' metacognitive skills will require a more consistent, intensive, and explicit attempt that will require practice, feedback, and strategies on a distributed basis within a course setting" (p. 22). Both studies are providing mandates for the Constructivist teacher; how does a Constructivist teacher embed metacognitive skills into the classroom?

14.2 Metacognition and Constructivism

The Constructivist teacher must carefully examine the process of incorporating metacognition into his classroom. Grossman (2009) discussed assignments for improving the ability for students to reflect. He presented a situation in which he gave his education students the opportunity to tutor in a local elementary school. To receive credit, students were expected to write reflective notes about the tutoring session and relate their experience to course concepts. Students, however, disappointed Grossman. "To my surprise, the first reflections were not really reflections at all," he wrote (p. 16). Instead of connecting what they observed with course theories, the students just described what they saw. In Constructivist terms, students did not "turn the kaleidoscope." Grossman cited Kegan (1994) as saying that "reflective thinking requires a mental place to stand apart for, or outside of, a durably created idea, thought, or description" (p. 275).

A similar idea comes from Zimmerman (2002), who states that self-regulation "involves the selective use of processes that must be personally adapted to each learning task" (p. 66). The process of adapting processes to new learning situations is consistent with creating a new construct. Consider the prompt that has been suggested several times in this book: "Discuss what confused you today." While this prompt can be an effective assessment instrument, it does risk becoming merely a descriptive exercise in which students just list points that confused them, without creating a possible strategy to address the difficulty. To make this prompt a Constructivist activity, the teacher could instead say, "Discuss what confused you today, and also describe the causes of the confusion. Was it the learning style? The mode of the presentation?"

For the Constructivist teacher, metacognition is more than just thinking about thinking. It is the process of *creating a new mental location or a new mental construct.*

14.3 Examples of Constructivist Metacognition

Presented here are examples of Constructivist metacognition. We use charts designated by the three components of Constructivist metacognition: cognition, academic tasks, and strategies.

TABLE 14.1 Cognition

Prompt	Constructivist Prompt
Discuss what teaching strategy helped you learn today.	Discuss what teaching helped you learn today and *why it helped.* (As an example: There were many comparative learning activities, and I learn when working with others. Another example: Many diagrams were presented, and I learn visually.)
Discuss what you learned today that surprised you.	Discuss what you learned today that surprised you and *why it surprised you* or what activity created that surprise. (As an example: When you put us in groups of four, the other three people all disagreed with me for the same reason. I was surprised, and I realized that I needed to change my thinking in that direction.)
Discuss what you learned today from your partner.	Discuss what you learned from your partner and discuss why you learned. (As an example, was it the way the explained it? Was it that their thinking represented a new perspective and by discussing this with them you changed your conceptual perspective?)

Next we look at the metacognitive component of *academic tasks.* Costa (1984) suggests that teachers encourage students to share their progress on the task, to ask questions concerning rules and parameters for the task, what else needs to be done, and so forth. In discussing self-regulated learning (SRL), Paris and Paris (2001) pointed to problem-based learning (PBL) as a tool that "teachers can utilize to support the development of SRL" (p. 94). PBL activities, as described in Chapter 13, provide an opportunity for students to develop metacognitive constructs.

TABLE 14.2 Academic Tasks and Strategies

Prompt	Constructivist Prompt
What needs to be done in this problem?	What do we need to learn to solve this problem? Rank these in order of importance, and be prepared to explain your reasoning.
How has today's lesson changed your thinking concerning this problem?	Discuss how the central focus of our PBL has changed, and be sure to include what activities or readings forced this change.
What have you learner today?	Discuss how you will implement at least one idea you learned today into the solution of the PBL scenario.
What have you learned today?	Discuss one idea from today's class that you will *not* use in the solution of the PBL. Be sure to discuss specific reasons for this.
Summarize today's reading.	Of the readings that we have covered so far, which one is the most important for your solution to the scenario? Be sure to explain your answer by referring to your philosophy of education or your philosophy of assessment.
Your group has four articles to read. Decide on how you will divide this reading up.	Write a reflection on the best strategy to review the four articles: (a) have all four people read them and then have a group discussion; or (b) have each person read one article, and then report out to the entire group. Be sure to briefly discuss how you would assess this strategy.
Come up with one idea for the solution that has not been covered in class.	According to the rubric, you are to use an idea for the solution that was not covered in class. Write a short reflection on what this idea is, why you chose it, on how to acquire the information, and how you will evaluate the importance of the information you find.

15

The Entire Process

While the examples from Chapter 13 provide some insight into the Constructivist philosophy in action through PBL, this chapter provides a thorough examination of the entire process. As a review, we graphically depict the process (see Figure 15.1).

15.1   Example from Sixth-Grade Mathematics

Now let's look at this process in action. Our example comes from the sixth-grade math class at Saint Ethelreda School in Chicago, Illinois. I have the pleasure of working with the middle-school students at this school on a weekly basis, together with the math teacher there, Mrs. Lillie Pass. Each class lasts 35 minutes, and the lesson presented here spanned a couple of days.

1. Teacher Planning

Since this example is taken from my work in Illinois, we need to understand the framework of the Illinois Learning Standards. The first component of this framework is the category of "Goals." Goals are broad statements of knowledge or skills that are the organizing agent of the subject matter.

The Comprehensive Handbook of Constructivist Teaching, pages 175–189
Copyright © 2010 by Information Age Publishing
All rights of reproduction in any form reserved.

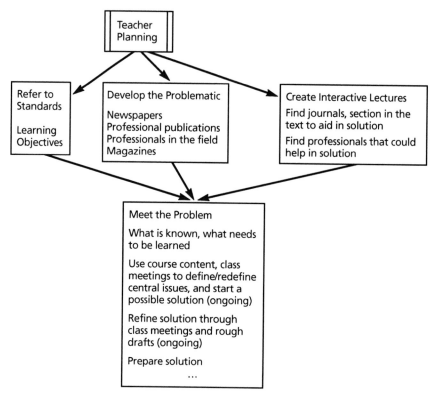

Figure 15.1

Each goal has an explanation with it that examines why the goal is important and how it is of value to the student beyond school. The next component is the "Learning Standard." A Learning Standard is a statement that describes a specific skill or knowledge within the goal. A goal will have several such learning standards that, taken together, represent the learning needed to fulfill that goal. "Learning Benchmarks" are indicators for monitoring student progress. Grade-level clusters are the Learning Benchmarks and are categorized as early elementary, late elementary, middle/junior high school, early high school, and late high school. Each learning area or content area has a section referred to as "Applications of Learning." In this section five cross-disciplinary abilities are discussed: solving problems, communicating, using technology, working on teams, and making connections.

Mrs. Pass and I examined the results from the previous year's standardized tests and decided that we wanted to empower students in the areas of geometric and spatial sense, with a focus on solving problem and communicating. Next, we considered goals and identified two goals that applied here. The first, State Goal 7, involves estimating; making and using measurements of objects, quantities, and relationships; and determining acceptable levels of accuracy. The Learning Benchmark in the middle/junior high school cluster that applies is 7.A.3a—Measure length, capacity, weight/mass and angles using sophisticated instruments (e.g., compass, protractor, trundle wheel). State Goal 9 also applies in this situation: using geometric methods to analyze, categorize, and draw conclusions about points, lines, planes, and spaces. The Learning Benchmarks in this case are as follows: 9.B.3—Identify, describe, classify and compare two-and three-dimensional geometric figures and models according to their properties; and 9.C.3a—Construct, develop and communicate logical arguments (informal proofs) about geometric figures and patterns.

The students were to study polygons—explicitly, the sums of the angles of polygons. Thus, at this stage of the planning, we had to come up with a lesson on the properties (angle sums) of polygons. To this end, I started to skim the newspapers to see what was going on in the real world. What I found was a world filled with lawsuits and court proceedings. I supplemented this information with a DVD of one of the seasons of the lawyer show "Perry Mason." The result is a lesson involving the sums of the angles of polygons in the context of a court trial.

2. Meet the Problem

We introduced the class to the problem with the following handout.

The Lawyer and a Geometry Problem

You are in a courtroom and are the lawyer for the defendant. The complainant's lawyer shows this diagram to the jury and the judge. What should you do and why?

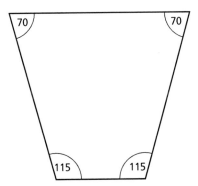

Figure 15.2

In order to create a sense of autonomy, the students were asked to write down their ideas first (Rattle their cage) and then share with their partners (Turn the kaleidoscope). More precisely, they were encouraged to consider what they know and what they needed to learn. Below are the results.

Know

- There is a jury and a judge.
- Everyone has a diagram.
- The diagram has two 115-degree angles on the bottom and two 70-degree angles on the top.

Need to Learn

- How do we know that the diagram is correct?
- Are the facts of math in line with the diagram?
- Does this type of figure exist?
- What type of figure is this?

The first question led to a discussion of how we know that something is true. The students wrote down what they thought and shared their ideas with their partner. Students then went to the board to write down what their partner said. The results are below.

- When the book tells us so.
- When the teacher tells us so.
- When we do it ourselves, that is, measure the angles ourselves.
- When the facts of geometry agree with the diagram.

We then added to our "Need to Learn" list two questions:

- How do we measure angles?
- What are the facts of geometry?

For the next phase, "gather information," we passed out the worksheet in Figure 15.3.

The students were asked how they might start to measure the angle. Our intention was to have the students develop autonomy and to activate their prior knowledge on the measurement of angles. As hints, we asked the following: "Let's look at angle A for the first problem on the worksheet. Where is the starting point of angle A? Why would you think that is the starting point?" We then modeled for students how to align the protractor. All of the students are given a protractor (Figure 15.4).

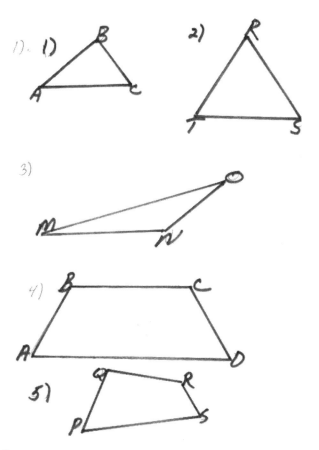

Figure 15.3

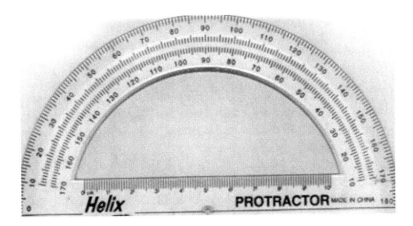

Figure 15.4

A student immediately asked, "What scale do we use?" Our response: "Think about what scale you think that we should use, and then compare your decision with that of your partner." Again, our intention was to have students start with what they know and reason from there.

In this case most of the students said to use the "inner scale," although they were not able to articulate why (in this case, "start with zero") and did not know that they could use the other scale (the scale starting with 180). So, we let them proceed. After the students measured angle A as 40 degrees, I said, "Hmmm . . . Let's use the outer scale for the fun of it. Where is the starting point? Ah, yes, 180. Now, what is the other number we use?" Obviously, my intention was to have the students realize that there is a second way to do this measurement. Also, since the numbers on this scale would go in the "opposite direction," there was a great opportunity to "Rattle their cage."

Some students said that the "other number" to use was "158"; other students were not sure. One student meekly threw out "142." My response: "Well, why is there silence? What is going on here? Let's look at the scale: 180, 170, and 160. . . . What can you say about the scale?" [*Here it is important for the students to create the concept and the words for the construct that the scale is decreasing.*] Now students did the computation for 180-142. Together, we modeled several examples of determining the measure of an angle using either scale.

To have the students participate in a debriefing phase, I asked them to write a few lines telling what they had learned that would help them solve the Lawyer Problem. Two typical answers were as follows: "I learned the measurements of an angle and facts of the diagram" and "I learned to ask about the diagram and to measure the angle to tell what the diagram is." Obviously, the students have not created a true construct, particularly regarding the use of the protractor. We used their responses as guidelines for the next stage of the activity.

3. Gather Information

We began the second class with a question: "Look at yesterday's list of things to learn. What items have we learned?" After a brief class discussion the following was put up on the board:

- How do we know that the diagram is correct?—We don't. We must determine this by measuring the angles in the diagram.
- How do we measure angles? We know this—but perhaps we better review the technique to gain more mastery.

- What are the facts of geometry? We do not know any facts about geometry yet.

Note that we are "Turning the kaleidoscope." The students are not just reviewing what has been done; they are creating a mental plan of what still needs to be done.

The remainder of the class was spent on ensuring that all students know how to measure angles by using a protractor. At the end of the class, again, we asked the question "How does what we learned today help us solve the Lawyer Problem? [*This question enables the student to create a "new mental space" by connecting the measuring of angles to solving the Lawyer Problem.*] The following represent some of the responses:

- When we measure the angles, we have facts.
- Our measurements show that the diagram is wrong.

We then had the class apply this knowledge by measuring the angles in the diagram of the Lawyer Problem and discover the incorrect measurement.

4. Interactive Lecture

The following version of the Interactive Lecture does not have a worksheet presented but does depict what happened. The students next were asked to write down the three most important things that they had learned from our work over the past few days. Typical answers focused on how to measure angles and how to know if a diagram is correct.

1. **Think/Pair/Share.** We will do a pair/share, but you are to write down what your partner says. [*This activity has multiple purposes. First, it empowers students to "Rattle their cage," or to make connections by listening to and writing down what another person says. Second, it provides an opportunity to hear another person discuss how to solve the Lawyer Problem. Third, it engages students in the lifelong skill of listening to another.*]
2. **Group of Four Consensus.** The students next were put in groups of four; each group discussed the ideas from the pair/share and decided what were the two most important ideas. [*This activity continues the enabling of students to make connections and to modify their thinking based on the responses of others.*]
3. **Class Share.** We then called on one student from each group to say what the two important ideas were; these were written on the board. One of the reappearing responses was "How to measure angles."

When asked "What has this to do with the Lawyer Problem? How does this help you show that the diagram is incorrect?" the class came to this consensus:

"During the court proceedings, we will actually measure the angles."

Another statement on the board was "Does the diagram agree with the facts?" When asked, "What facts are we talking about?" the class was silent. We provided a hint: "Well, in court the opposing attorney would probably ask for some geometric facts to compare to the diagram. What fact have we come up with?" Again, silence.

4. **What Was Learned.** Our natural inclination was simply to tell the students that the sum of the angles of a triangle equal 180 degrees and to verify that with their diagrams. Wanting the students to create their own knowledge, we instead suggested, "Get with a partner and write down all that you know about triangles." One of the conclusions was that the sum of the three angles was 180 degrees. How did they know? Most of the responses were of the sort "We just know that" or "It is in the book." We reminded the class that they need other ways to accept facts. And looking at examples of their measurements, the students did just that. After a discussion concerning how "thickness of the side of the triangle or the thickness of the marking on the protractor may make a difference," the class created their own version of the statement that the three angles of a triangle equal 180 degrees.

5. Triangles and Number Families

To have the students make more connections by "Turning the kaleidoscope," we introduced a visual representation of equations, loosely referred to as "number families." Below is an example.

"Let's look at the three numbers 9, 6, and 15. Can we use addition and subtraction to create some number facts?" This results in the following "family of number facts."

$$9 + 6 = 15$$
$$6 + 9 = 15$$
$$15 - 9 = 6$$
$$15 - 6 = 9.$$

We then put a diagram on the board (Figure 15.5):

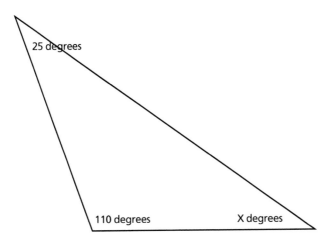

Figure 15.5

The students were asked to create a "family of facts" about this triangle using addition and subtraction. This activity represented a double version of "Rattling their cage." First, since the three angles total 180 degrees, there are four numbers, and up to now the class was involved in using just three numbers; second, one of the numbers was a variable. Many students would say things such as $x = 110 + 25$, probably because students go through school learning that "x means get the answer." A short discussion led students to create the construct of simplifying numbers so that they ended up with the following:

$$135 + x = 180$$
$$x + 135 = 180$$
$$180 - x = 135$$
$$180 - 135 = x.$$

This exercise is important, not only because it presents a situation for connecting and modifying a previous learning scheme, but because it connects the cognitive scheme of number families and modifies that scheme by presenting a situation where the facts include a variable that does not represent "getting the answer." Moreover, the exercise requires students to simplify expressions. An activity such as this provides multiple opportunities to "Turn the kaleidoscope."

6. Triangles and the Figure in the Lawyer Problem

Once again, to "Turn the Kaleidoscope," we asked the students to get into groups and discuss how they could use their knowledge about triangles to solve the Lawyer Problem. Figure 15.6 shows some examples of the work turned in.

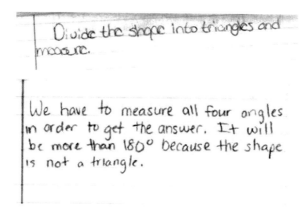

Divide the shape into triangles and measure.

We have to measure all four angles in order to get the answer. It will be more than 180° because the shape is not a triangle.

Figure 15.6

An analysis of these responses indicates that the students have worked together to create some mental constructs that will help in solving the Lawyer Problem. In the first example, students actually show what they will do; while this diagram is not correctly drawn (it includes an angle from a triangle not in the trapezoid), it does represent prior knowledge that can be used. The second example says this in words, and the third brings out the fact that the answer will be greater than 180 degrees.

The next day when the students came into the classroom, they saw the following on the board:

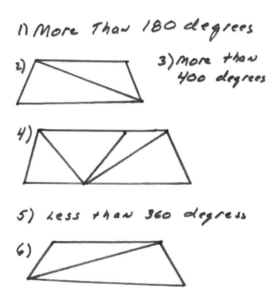

1) More Than 180 degrees

2)

3) More than 400 degrees

4)

5) Less than 360 degress

6)

Figure 15.7

The students were asked, "Which of these diagram or phrase would you not use?"

[*This exercise is intended to connect to their previous knowledge that the three angles of a triangle measure 180 degrees, that the four angles of a trapezoid measure more than 180 degrees, and that to determine the sum of the angles of a quadrilateral, one divides the quadrilateral into triangles. The first example is used to activate the scheme that the sum of the angles of a quadrilateral will be more than the sum of the angles of a triangle. The second and third examples are used to activate the scheme that the "direction" of the diagonal is unimportant. The third example is intended to "Rattle their cage" by inserting the idea that the angles formed by the triangles only represent the angles of the trapezoid.*]

Students eventually came to a consensus on what geometry facts they had constructed.

There remained, however, some confusion whether a trapezoid exists. Students argued that even though they could draw one, this did not necessarily prove it existed. This class was therefore given time to find examples in the room. When numerous examples in the room were found, the class agreed that a trapezoid existed and that they could refer to these in the trial, if need be. This activity resulted in the following "geometry facts" constructed by the class.

- The angles of a triangle add up to 180 degrees.
- A trapezoid exists but often it is "flipped."
- A trapezoid can be split up into two triangles.
- The angles of a trapezoid add up to 360 degrees.
- You can "prove" things about the measures of a triangle or trapezoid through logic or through direct measuring.

7. The Trial Day

On the day of the trial, "Judge Pelech" convened the court, and the prosecution's lawyer, "Attorney Pass," started by presenting her case that the diagram was correct. Students acted as a team of lawyers. They presented their case by going to the board and discussing how to measure an angle and by using the "geometry facts" that they had constructed. It is important to know that this activity was made to be as real as possible. I wore my graduation gown, and we actually had one student act as a bailiff.

[*This "trial" represents the concept of role playing/drama and authentic situations rolled into one. The students had to demonstrate and apply their mathematical knowledge in a "real" setting. This is an example of "TV reality show."*]

15.2 Analysis of the Sixth-Grade Example

The planning for this lesson started by blending the state standards with an authentic situation; the mathematical knowledge students were expected to know by the state was embedded in and connected to a real-life situation. Students created the necessary knowledge by formulating their own questions through the know/need to know technique (Captain of their own ship). This knowledge was refined through interaction with other students (Rattle their cage and turn the Kaleidoscope) and involved the spoken word, the written word, the visual mode, and the kinesthetic mode. Many of the class activities were guided by the Interactive Lecture. The final product of this lesson was presenting the case in front of a judge.

15.3 Example from a College Measurement and Evaluation Class

Our second example comes from Chapter 13. In this scenario a practicing administrator, through a conference call, discusses with students what a new teacher needs to know about assessment during the first two weeks of school. To provide a Constructivist framework, I assigned the article "Assessing What Matters" (Sternberg, 2007/2008) I told the students that they must find what really matters: people skills, application of content, creative thinking, not memorizing. I put students in groups, assigned one of the findings, and asked each group to write out on chart paper their beliefs. Thus, I revamped the Interactive Lecture presented in Chapter 13. This is the point where our discussion will begin. The following represents portions of the interactive lecture. While the lesson did not provide an actual handout, the lesson did follow the format and sequence presented. Directions or prompts that would be printed on the handout were either said or written on the board (or both).

1. **Group assignment.**   Get with your partner. You will be assigned a topic from either our list on the board or the text. You will then write out on chart paper your outcomes and two ways in which you will assess these outcomes.

    [These all represent domains that are not usually officially assessed and/or cannot be assessed with traditional pencil and papers tests, and represent a "rattling their cage" and a new "turn of the kaleidoscope."]

    The charts are put up in various parts of the room, with one group standing in front of each chart. At a signal, all student groups rotate clockwise to the next sheet. They are given a few minutes to copy down the ideas of other students and then again rotate.

2. **Purposes of assessment.**   The students are asked to write down one idea they got from the activity and explain how that activity can be formative, diagnostic, or so forth. *[While students are being autonomous here, they are also making connections to the thoughts of others.]* Some of the actual responses follow:

- Assess on how students apply content.
- Creative writing.
- Not memorizing.
- Wisdom.
- Lifelong skills.
- People skills.

Since some of the ideas were broad, such as wisdom and lifelong skills, I used cooperative learning activities and a whole group discussion to break these categories down into more concrete, observable behaviors.

3. **Wild Card.**   Here students become "Captain of their ship" by suggesting what should come next. One result of the "Wild Card" approach in this class was a detailed discussion on placement assessment in the daily activities of the classroom teacher.

15.4   An Alternative Approach to College Measurement and Evaluation Class

Let's look at another approach to the same class and same scenario. The only handout given in this class was the following one; there was no handout outlining the sequence of events.

INTERACTIVE LECTURE ON PHILOSOPHY OF ASSESSMENT

WHAT WILL YOU ASSESS? TYPES OF ASSESSMENT/PURPOSES OF
ASSESSMENT/ROLES DURING ASSESSMENT

DR. PELECH

EDUC

NAME _____

1. **Look at the list of assessment tools below. Get in pairs, and put these tools into three groups. Be prepared to explain your reasoning.**
   A. Having students do practice ACT (ISAT) questions.
   B. Having students name the three main characters from the first three chapters of a novel they read the night before.

C. Having students compare and contrast the Civil War with the Bosnian by writing a short article for the local newspaper.

D. The teacher roaming around and listening to students work together as a team.

E. Having students solve an equation such as $3x - 4 = 48$ by showing all of the steps.

F. Observing how a student interacts working with a student that he does not particularly like.

G. A student explaining in P.E. class how to lay down a bunt.

H. Having a student explain in a short presentation his views on an important social issue.

I. A teacher observing how soon a student gives up on solving a difficult problem.

J. Watching how patient a student is with another student that she is explaining a problem to.

K. Having students come up and explain to the teacher a timeline they developed for finishing a long-term project.

L. Having a student write a "Toll Booth Problem" about if or how their attitude toward (you name the subject) has changed.

M. Conducting a debate on whether war is ever necessary.

N. Having students discuss how the class can do something for the people at a nursing home.

O. Having students from Assessment Measures class complete a fill-in-the blank test.

P. Students in your class fill out an interest survey.

[This exercise enables students to use their autonomy to activate their prior knowledge or to create a version of prior knowledge. Here students will begin the process of classifying assessments by purpose or format. Teachers obviously have the option to have students classify into groups. This activity represents Captain of Their Ship, Turning the Kaleidoscope, and TV Reality Show.]

2. **Class Share**

[Here students are told to put their classifications on the board. Then the students who did not put it on the board must explain the reasoning. The teacher then blends the classifications with the book's definitions of placement assessment, formative assessment, summative assessment, and diagnostic assessment. This activity begins the process of creating a network of ideas regarding the purposes of assessment as opposed to the "traditional way" of directly lecturing about it or directly referring to the book's definition.]

3. **Application.** Imagine that you are an 8th grade Biology Honors teacher. Write down two examples of how you would use place-

ment assessment in your class. Discuss this with your partner and then decide on two activities that are the most representative in your opinion.

[This activity enables students to continue to create a network of connections and opportunities for "Turning the Kaleidoscope" and "Rattling Their Cage" (each other's cage).]

4. **Class Share and Explanation.** One person from each group will come to the board, and then the other partner will explain and lead a short discussion on what they put down on the board.

[By having the entire class look at the ideas of other students, all students are given the opportunity to have their cage rattled. Any ensuing discussion will enable students to make more connections.]

15.5   Summary

Let's look at what was going on here. First, course or State Standards are embedded into an authentic situation. Students are then immersed into the authentic situation by engaging in the know/need to know exercises, and they work on the solution through the Interactive Lecture. This provides the platform for implementing the Constructivist activities discussed throughout this book. Key to the success of the activity is their discussions and findings to the solution of the authentic situation. Not to do so would result in having class activities remain as isolated facts. Toll Booth passes, reflections, and graphic organizers can be used to ensure success.

16

Professional Resources for the Constructivist Teacher

The principles, strategies, and activities presented in this book should apply, not only to the students whom we are privileged to teach, but to ourselves as professionals who are dedicated to learn more about the process of helping others learn. This chapter focuses on helping you, the Constructivist educator, begin the *process* of creating a personal professional development program.

16.1 Basic Principles

Wiggins and McTighe (2006) stated that "instruction is most effective when it is personalized" (p. 29). Thus, you are encouraged not to take what is in this book as verbatim but to use these ideas as a reference point for creating your own principles and professional development program. The question then is "What is meant by the word 'professional'?" Again, Wiggins and McTighe provided some insights. They presented four characteristics of professionals:

The Comprehensive Handbook of Constructivist Teaching, pages 191–200
Copyright © 2010 by Information Age Publishing
All rights of reproduction in any form reserved.

1. Professionals act on the current knowledge in their field.
2. Professionals focus on meeting the needs of the people they serve.
3. Professionals are results-oriented.
4. Professionals measure themselves against the standards of their profession.

The first point, "current knowledge," challenges Constructivist educators to find and integrate core knowledge into their practice. What are the resources for determining this? The answer comes in the form of Constructivist organizations, web sites, and publications.

What exactly is the nature of this core knowledge? The second point answers this question: For the Constructivist educator, core knowledge is the knowledge of how a teacher can create an environment in which all students can become autonomous and create their own version of knowledge. What is the concrete manifestation of this knowledge? What does the Constructivist teacher concretely do to focus on the needs of the student? Wiggins and McTighe provided some foundations for the questions that the Constructivist teacher must answer. These are reworked to create the following "core questions":

1. What is working for students? What isn't working?
2. What content area are students struggling with?
3. What teaching strategies worked for certain groups, and not for others?
4. What can I, as the designer of the learning environment, control so all students can learn?
5. What forms of knowledge are students adept at creating?
6. What authentic products can be used to enable the student to learn?
7. What connections can students easily make? Which ones can't they make?
8. What activities provide an autonomous environment for students?
9. What questions should be asked in order for students to make connections? What do these questions entail?

When examining publications and web sites and in professional conversations, the Constructivist educator must guide all inquiry through the use of these questions.

The third point, results-oriented, acknowledges that the Constructivist educator must be continuously mindful of creating results. An instrument that can focus the Constructivist on results is action research. Action research can be used to address some of the core questions. Educational action research is research in which the teacher/instructor designs the research, collects data, interprets the data, and develops an action plan based on the data interpretation in order to improve teaching and improve student learning. This is in comparison to research that is done by an outside researcher.

The rest of this chapter examines resources that can be used to help Constructivist educators put the word "professional" into their practice.

16.2   Constructivist Organizations

The Association for Constructivist Teaching.   The Association for Constructivist Teaching is an organization that believes Constructivist teaching provides a rich, problem-solving arena that offers students the opportunity to explore and investigate. The organization is dedicated to fostering these principles. Association members live in America, Brazil, Mexico, China, and Australia. Members include classroom teachers, administrators, college and university personnel, researchers, and educational consultants. Benefits for being a member include *The Constructivist*, an educational e-journal and journal archive. Members also receive discounts on registration fees and early notice for a call for presenters. Here is the web site address: http://www.odu.edu/educ/act/conf.html.

The Institute for Learning Centered Education.   This organization provides online courses, strategies, quotes, and a newsletter and sponsors an outstanding summer conference. This conference, the *Constructivist Design Conference*, immerses the participant not only in theory but also in a practical project. This hands-on conference presents speakers and the opportunity to develop a product that can be used in one's practice. This conference presents an excellent platform for groups of teachers from the same school to work together. The Institute also has an excellent journal, the *Journal for the Practical Application of Constructivist Theory in Education*. This peer-reviewed journal has articles on theory and research and on the practical application of Constructivist theory in the classroom.

16.3   Books on Constructivism

This section provides information on some books that the Constructivist educator will be interested in. This list, by no means exhaustive, can get you started on the journey of developing an effective library. The books are presented in alphabetical order of the authors.

Title: *In Search of Understanding: The Case for Constructivist Classrooms*
Authors: Jacqueline Grennon Brooks and Marin G. Brooks
Publisher: Association for Supervision and Curriculum Development
Year: 1993

> This book is as vital to the Constructivist library as pitching is to baseball. The book presents the case and foundations for establishing Constructivist practices in the classroom. The chapter "Becoming a Constructivist Teacher" provides important guidelines for the Constructivist practitioner.

Title: *Schooling for Life: Reclaiming the Essence of Learning*
Author: Jacqueline Grennon Brooks
Publisher: Association for Supervision and Curriculum Development
Year: 2002

> This book is a must for every Constructivist. The book focuses on how to make the school a place in which students are engaged in solving problems that are relevant to them. Brooks' own words describe the importance of this book: "This book is about how we might, in the name of progress, blur the distinctions between 'school life' and 'real life', between learning and teaching, between learning well and living well" (p. ix).

Title: *Toward a Theory of Instruction*
Author: Jerome S. Bruner
Publisher: The Belknap Press of Harvard University
Year: 1963 (4th Printing)

> Written in 1967 by one of the great writers in the field of education, this book presents challenges and themes for all Constructivist educators to examine. Bruner sets the groundwork for developing one's Constructivist philosophy. He examines how children learn and how they can be helped to learn.

Title: *The Process of Education*
Author: Jerome S. Bruner
Publisher: Vintage Books
Year: 1963

> This is an extremely influential book that represents Bruner's sense of a meeting at Woods Hole on Cape Cod in 1959 that brought together thirty-five scientists, educators, and scholars to discuss how science education could be improved.

Title: *Constructivist Strategies: Meeting Standards and Engaging Adolescent Minds*
Authors: Chandra J. Foote, Paul J. Vermette, and Catherine F. Battaglia
Publisher: Eye on Education
Year: 2001

> Presenting theory, implications and examples of how to use Constructivist theory to create a student-centered classroom, this book is in an easily understandable format.

Title: *Applying Standards-Based Constructivism: A Two-Step Guide for Motivating Middle and High School Students*
Authors: Pat Flynn, Don Mesibov, Paul J. Vermette, R. Michael Smith
Publisher: Eye on Education
Year: 2004

> This practical book combines the Constructivist theory and philosophy with applications in the classroom. This book is easy for the practitioner to read and is an excellent reference.

Title: *Constructivism: Theory, Perspectives, and Practice* (2nd ed.)
Editor: Catherine Twomey Fosnot
Publisher: Teachers College Press
Year: 2005

> The second edition of this book builds on the success of the best-selling first edition. Included are chapters on theory, perspectives from Constructivism in different disciplines, and Constructivism in disability studies. Contributors include Ernst von Glaserfeld, Paul Cobb, and Maxine Greene.

Title: Cooperative Learning
Author: Spencer Kagan
Publisher: Kagan Publishing
Year: 1994

> This excellent book discusses cooperative learning activities that will provide a Constructivist environment for any classroom. The book also provides guidance for the teacher.

Title: *Young Children Reinvent Arithmetic: Implications of Piaget's Theory* (2nd ed.)
Author: Constance Kamii with Leslie Baker Housman
Publisher: Teachers College Press
Year: 2000

This compelling book describes practical suggestions and activities that can be used to empower students to construct their mathematical thinking. An embedded theme is that children are much more capable than what adults believe.

Title: *Young Children Continue to Reinvent Arithmetic—3rd Grade: Implications of Piaget's Theory*
Author: Constance Kamii with Sally Jones Livingston
Publisher: Teachers College Press
Year: 1994

In this book, Kamii continues her examination of Piaget's theory. In collaboration with Sally Jones Livingston, Kamii examines what third-grade children do when they solve problems.

Title: *How People Learn* (Expanded ed.)
Author: National Research Council
Publisher: National Academy Press
Year: 2000

This excellent book looks at how people learn and presents implications for what we teach, and how it should be taught.

Title: *Problems as Possibilities: Problem-based Learning for K–16* (2nd ed.)
Authors: Linda Torp and Sara Sage
Publisher: Association for Supervision and Curriculum Development
Year: 2002

Problem-based learning (PBL) is examined thoroughly from several perspectives. The book includes theory on PBL, examples from all levels of education, and chapters on design and implementation.

Titles: *Activators: Activities to Engage Students' Thinking before Instruction*
Summarizers: Activity Structures to Support Integration and Retention of New Learning
Authors: Jon Saphier and Mary Ann Haley
Publisher: Research for Better Teaching, Inc.
Year: 1993

These companion books provide many activities that not only call up prior knowledge before a topic is studied; they also provide activities that get students to actively summarize what they have learned. The Constructivist teacher will find that these books provide activities that readily blend with Constructivist theory.

16.4   Web Sites

This section lists a few sites that will help the Constructivist teacher start a library and get started implementing the Constructivist philosophy.

1. The Problem-Based Learning Network at the Illinois Mathematics and Science Academy: http://pbln.imsa.edu . This web site is a must for anyone interested in using PBL. Among its contents are research articles and a detailed analysis of the PBL model.
2. Lunar Outpost Coaching Learning Experience Design: http://pbln.imsa.edu/model/problems/lunar2008/led/intro/index.html . This is an online unit for coaching a PBL unit.
3. USA TODAY: http://www.usatoday.com/educate/lessons.htm. This web site has lesson plans that bring real-world issues into the classroom.
4. The Association for Conceptual Study: http://www.conceptualstudy.org/. This web site is maintained by Richard Singer, who has worked with me on the Bridging Question Strategy (BQS). One of the links on this web site is dedicated to Constructivism.

16.5   Action Research

Action research is another component of professional development for the Constructivist educator because it is the embodiment of the four principles of professionalism presented at the beginning of the chapter. First, let us define what action research is. While there are many definitions of action research, there are some commonalities for educational action research:

1. It is systematic inquiry.
2. It is done by the teacher or administrator (stakeholder).
3. It is done while the teacher is teaching.
4. The purpose is to improve the learning of the students/pedagogy of the teacher.
5. The results are analyzed to create a plan of action for improving the learning of students/pedagogy of the teacher.

Action research aligns with the four characteristics of professionals. Not only does the Constructivist teacher act on current knowledge, he is creating current knowledge. Action research aligns with the second component, fulfilling the needs of the people served by looking at ways to increase student learning. Action research is results-oriented (the third component):

the results are not only analyzed but acted upon. Since action research is intended to help the profession directly, it actually is a component of the standards of the profession.

16.5.1   Resources for Action Research

The following resources will help with constructing a mental template of action research.

Title: *Guiding School Improvement with Action Research*
Author: Richard Sagor
Publisher: Association for Supervision and Curriculum Development.
Year: 2000

> This book defines action research and analyzes the process in detail. It provides a detailed, but readable platform.

Title: *Action Research: A Guide for the Teacher Researcher* (2nd ed.)
Author: Geoffrey E. Mills
Publisher: Merrill Prentice Hall
Year: 2003

> Action research is defined by this book, which also provides theory and a historical backdrop. The action research process is thoroughly discussed.

Teacher Research: http://www.accessexcellence.org/LC/TL/AR/index.php. This web site, maintained by Sharon Parsons, provides an easy-to-read format of understanding the nature of action research.

16.5.2   An Example of Action Research for the Constructivist Teacher

What follows is a glimpse of the Action Research I have conducted at Saint Ethelreda School in Illinois. The purpose of the research was to determine how *students* view the effectiveness of Constructivist activities.

Description of the Study: *Examining How Middle School Math Students Perceive Their Learning Processes*

Overview

This Action Research study examines the metacognitive processes of Middle School Math Students at Saint Ethelreda School in Chicago, Illinois. The population of this study numbers approximately eighty students. Saint Ethelreda and Benedictine University are in a partnership in which

Benedictine University School of Education Faculty and Administrators work with the student body and administration in modeling best practices.

Research Questions

This study examines the following three research questions:

1. In the view of Saint Ethelreda Middle School math students, what Constructivist teaching strategies are most effective?
2. In the view of Saint Ethelreda Middle School math students, what are the reasons for the effectiveness of these strategies?
3. What is the relationship between student rankings of strategies and academic achievement?

Mechanics

Each week the principal investigator (Dr. Pelech) will model best practices in each of the middle school math classes. This modeling by Dr. Pelech will be done at least once a week during the fall semester. This modeling will be videotaped for purposes of examining the mechanics of Dr. Pelech's delivery. The best practice activities will come from the following pool:

1. Cooperative learning activities.
2. Constructivist reading activities.
3. Authentic writing activities.
4. Problem-based learning activities.

Dr. Pelech plans to use one activity from the above categories. Mrs. Pass, the math teacher and the other investigator, will then also implement the activity for the students. At the end of the week, Dr. Pelech will ask students to write a reflection on the week's activity (this instrument is also included in a separate attachment). The prompts for this reflection will be as follows:

1. In your own words, briefly describe the activity that Dr. Pelech modeled and used, and that was also used by Mrs. Pass.
2. Look at the following statement. "This week's activity helped me learn mathematics." Please circle the response that describes how you feel.

    Strongly agree   Agree   Disagree   Strong Disagree

3. Look at your response from above. Write a few sentences to explain why you feel the way you do about the activity.

Each week Dr. Pelech and Mrs. Pass will review student responses and summarize them by doing the following:

- Using descriptive statistics to examine the responses to question 2.
- Coding the responses to question 3 and using descriptive statistics to describe them.
- Obtaining Terra Nova scores for each student and correlating them with the responses to questions 2 and 3.

At the end of three weeks, the students will be asked to rank the three activities they have experienced and to briefly discuss their rankings. The prompts are below (and are also in another attachment).

Dr. Pelech has just reviewed the learning activities from the last three weeks. He has written their names on the board. Please rank these by writing the name of the activity in each blank. The first blank is for the activity that is the most effective for you. Underneath please explain why it was the most effective for you. The second blank is for the second most effective activity. Underneath please explain why it was the second most effective for you. The third blank is for the activity that was the third most effective activity. Underneath please explain why you ranked it third.

    1. *Most Effective Activity for you* _____
    2. *Second Most Effective Activity for you* _____
    3. *Third Most Effective Activity for you* _____

Dr. Pelech and Mrs. Pass will then examine the results using descriptive statistics.

References

Abbott, M. L., & Fouts, J. T. (Eds.). (2003). *Constructivist teaching and student achievement: The results of a school-level classroom observation study in Washington* (Technical Report #5). Lynnwood: Washington School Research Center.

Aburime, F. D. (2007). How manipulatives affect the mathematics achievement of students in Nigerian schools. *Educational Research Quarterly, 31*(1), 3–16.

Airasian, P. W., & Walsh, M. E. (1997). Constructivist cautions. *Phi Delta Kappan,* 444–449.

Albanese, M. A., & Mitchell, S. (1993). Problem-based learning. *Academic Medicine, 68*(1), 52–81.

Alesandrini, K. (2002). Visual constructivism in distance learning. *USDLA Journal.* Retrieved August 23, 2008, from: www.usdla.org/html/journal/JAN02-Issue/artcile03.html.

Alvermann, D. E. (1981). The compensatory effect of graphic organizers on descriptive text. *Journal of Educational Research, 75*(1), 44–48.

Anderson, K. M. (2007). Differentiating instruction to include all students. *Preventing School Failure, 51*(3), 49–54.

Annis, L. F. (1981). Effect of preference for assigned lecture notes on student achievement. *Journal of Educational Research, 74*(3), 179–182.

Applebee, A .N., Langer, J. A., Nystrand, N., & Gamoran, A. (2003). Discussion-based approaches to developing understanding: Classroom instruction and student performance in middle and high school English. *American Educational Research Journal, 40*(3), 685–730.

Araujo, U. (1996). *A longitudinal approach to the relations between the "cooperative school environment" and children's moral judgment.* Unpublished manuscript, Unicamp/Brasil.

The Comprehensive Handbook of Constructivist Teaching, pages 201–215

Aschner, M. J., Gallagher, J. J., Perry, J. M. & Asfar, S. F. (1961). *A system for classifying thought processes in the context of classroom verbal interaction.* Urbana: University of Illinois.

Association for Conceptual Study. Maintained by Richard Singer. http://www.conceptualstudy.org/.

Association for Constructivist Teaching: http://www.odu.edu/educ/act/conf.html.

Au, K. H., & Carroll, J. H. (1997). Improving literacy achievement through a constructivist approach: The KEEP demonstration classroom project. *The Elementary School Journal, 97*(3), 203–221.

Bacon, E. H., & Bloom. L. A. (1995). Beyond the herring sandwich phenomenon: A holistic constructivist approach to teacher education. *Journal of Learning Disabilities, 28*(10), 636–645.

Baggini, J., & Stangroom, J. (Eds.). (2004). *Great thinkers A-Z: 2,5000 years of thought that shaped the western world.* New York: MJF Books.

Bartlett, F. C. (1997). *Thinking: A study in experimental and social psychology* (3rd printing). New York: Cambridge University Press.

Bean, T. W., Searles, D., Singer, & Cowen, S. (1990). Learning concepts from biology text through pictorial analogies and an analogical study guide. *Journal of Educational Research, 83*(4), 233–237.

Becker, K. H., & Maunsaiyat, S. (2004). A comparison of students' achievement and attitudes between constructivist and traditional classroom environments in Thailand vocational electronics programs. *Journal of Vocational Education Research, 29*(2), 133–153.

Bentley, J. E. (1958). *Philosophy: An outline-history.* Ames, IA: Littlefield, Adams & Co.

Beyer, B. K. (2008). What research tells us about teaching thinking skills. *The Social Studies, 99*(5), 7–29.

Blackburn, D. W., Bonvillian, J. D., & Ashby, R. P. (1984, January). Manual communication as an alternative mode of language instruction for children with severe reading disabilities. *Language, Speech, and Hearing Services in Schools.*

Boon, R. T., Fiore, C., & Spencer, V. G. (2007). Teachers' attitudes and perceptions toward the use of Inspiration 6 software in inclusive world history classes at the secondary level. *Journal of Instructional Psychology, 34*(3), 166–171.

Booth, D. (1985). "Imaginary gardens with real toads": Reading and drama in education. *Electronic Theory Into Practice, 24*(3), 193–198.

Boulware-Gooden, R., Carreker, S., Thornhill, A., & Joshi, R. M. (2007). Instruction of metacognitive strategies enhances reading comprehension and vocabulary achievement of third-grade students. *The Reading Teacher, 61*(1), 70–77.

Bowen, C. W. (2000). A quantitative literature review of cooperative learning effects on high school and college chemistry achievement. *Journal of Chemical Education, 77*(1), 116–119.

Brooks, J. (2002). *Schooling for life: Reclaiming the essence of learning.* Alexandria, VA: Association for Supervision and Curriculum Development.

Brooks, J. B., & Brooks, M. (1993). *In search of understanding: The case for constructivist classrooms.* Alexandria, VA: Association for Supervision and Curriculum Development.

Brown, J. S., Collins, A. & Duguid, P. (1989). Situated cognition and the culture of learning. *Educational Researcher, 18,* 32–42.

Bruner, J. S. (1963). *The process of education* (6th ed.). New York: Vintage Books.

Bruner, J. S. (1967). *Toward a theory of instruction.* Cambridge, MA: The Belknap Press of Harvard University Press.

Bruning, R., & Horn, C. (2000). Developing motivation to write. *Educational Psychologist, 35*(1), 25–37.

Burmark, L. (2002). *Visual literacy: Learn to see. See to learn.* Alexandria, VA: Association for Supervision and Curriculum Development.

Butcher, K. R. (2006). Learning from text with diagrams. Promoting mental model development and inference generation. *Journal of Educational Psychology, 98*(1), 182–197.

Caine, R. N., & Caine, G. (1991). *Making connections: Teaching and the human brain.* Alexandria, VA: Association for Supervision and Curriculum Development.

Camahalan, F. M. (2006). Effects of a metacognitive reading program on the reading achievement and metaconitive strategies of students with cases of dyslexia. *Reading Improvement, 43*(2), 77–92.

Case, R. (1991). Advantages and limitations of the neo-Piagetian position. In R. Case (Ed.), *The mind's staircase: Exploring the conceptual underpinnings of children's thought and knowledge* (pp. 37–51). Hillsdale, NJ: Lawrence Erlbaum Associates.

Cass, M., Cates, D., Smith, M., & Jackson, C. (2003). Effects of manipulative instruction on solving area and perimeter problems by students with learning disabilities. *Learning Disabilities Research & Practice, 18*(2), 112–120.

Chang, K., Sung, Y., & Chen, I. (2002). The effect of concept mapping to enhance text comprehension and summarization. *The Journal of Experimental Education, 71*(1), 5–23.

Cheung, L. S. (2006). A constructivist approach to designing computer supported concept-mapping environment. *International Journal of Instructional Media, 33*(2), 153–164.

Christenbury, L., & Kelly, P. (1983). *Questioning: A path to critical thinking.* Urbana, IL: ERIC Clearinghouse on Reading and Communication Skills and the National Council of Teachers of English.

Clark, J. (2008, Winter). PowerPoint and pedagogy: Maintaining student interest in university lectures. *College Teaching, 56*(1), 39–44.

Comer, S. K. (2005). Patient care simulations. *Nursing Education Perspectives, 26*(6), 357–361.

Connell, J. D. (2005). *Brain-based strategies to reach every learner.* New York: Scholastic.

Consortium of National Arts Education Associations. (n.d.). National Standards for Arts Education.

Cooney, W., Cross, C., & Trunk, B. (1993). *From Plato to Piaget: The greatest educational theorists from across the centuries and around the world.* New York: University Press of America.

Cosenza, G. (2006). Play me a picture: Paint me a song: Integrating music learning with visual art. *General Music Today, 19*(2), 7–11. [Retrieved from the Internet on September 8, 2008.]

Costa , A. L. (1984). Mediating the metacognitive. *Educational Leadership, 42*(3), 57–62.

DeVries, R. (2002). *What does research on constructivist education tell us about effective schooling?* (The Iowa Academy of Education Occasional Research Paper #5) Des Moines, IA: First in the Nation in Education Foundation.

Dewey, J. (1991). *How we think.* Amherst, NY: Prometheus Books.

Diamond, M., & Hopson, J. (1998). *Magic trees of the mind.* New York: Penguin Group.

Dillon, J. T. (1984). Research on questioning and discussion. *Educational Leadership, 42*(3), 50–56.

DiPippa, J. M., & Peters, M. M. (2003). The lawyering process: An example of metacognition at its best. *Clinical Law Review, 10* (31), 311–325.

Dolk, M., Uittenbogaard, W., & Fosnot, C. T. (1997). *Teaching to facilitate progressive schematization.* Alexandria, VA: Association for Supervision and Curriculum Development.

Doolittle, P. E. (1997). Vygotsky's zone of proximal development as a theoretical foundation for cooperative learning. *Journal on Excellence in College Teaching, 8*(1), 83–103.

Doymus, K. (2007). Effects of a cooperative learning strategy on teaching and learning phases of matter and one-component phase diagrams. *Journal of Chemical Education, 8*(11), 1857–1860.

Druyan, S. (1997). Effect of the kinesthetic conflict on promoting scientific reasoning. *Journal of Research in Science Education, 34*(10), 1083–1099.

Duke, N. K., Purcell-Gates, V.P. Hall, L.A., & Tower, C. (2006/2007). Authentic literacy activities for developing comprehension and writing. *The Reading Teacher, 60*(4), 344–355.

Duraisingh, L. D., & Mansilla, V.B. (2007, December). Interdisciplinary forays within the history classroom: How the visual arts can enhance (or hinder) historical understanding. *Teaching History, 129,* 22–30.

Einstein, G. O., Morris, J. & Smith, S. (1985). Note-taking, individual differences, and memory for lecture information. *Journal of Educational Psychology, 77*(5), 522–532.

Eskew, M. (2006). Education in the age of globalism. *EDUEXEC. 25*(2), 6–7.

Fauconnier, G. (1997). *Mappings in thought and language.* New York: Cambridge University Press.

Favre, C., & Bizzini, L. (1995). Some contributions of Piaget's genetic epistemology and psychology to cognitive therapy. *Clinical Psychology and Psychotherapy, 2*(1), 15–23.

Fischer, K., & Rose, S. (1998, November). Growth cycles of brain and mind. *Educational Leadership,* 56–60.

Flavell, J. H. (1979). Metacognition and cognitive monitoring: A new area of cognitive-developmental inquiry. *American Psychologist, 34*(10), 906–911.

Flynn, P., Mesibov, D., Vermette, P. J., & Smith, R. M. (2004). *Applying standards-based constructivism: A two-step guide for motivating middle and high school students.* Larchmont, NY: Eye on Education.

Fogarty, R. (1999). Architects of the intellect. *Educational Leadership, 57*(3), 76–78.

Foote, C. J., Vermette, P. J., & Battaglia, C. F. (2001). *Constructivist strategies: Meeting standards and engaging adolescent minds.* Larchmont, NY: Eye on Education.

Fosnot, C. T., & Dolk, M. (2001). *Young mathematicians at work: Constructing multiplication and division.* Portsmouth, NH: Heinemann.

Fosnot, C. T., & Perry, R. (2005). Constructivism: A psychological theory of learning. In C. T. Fosnot (Ed.), *Constructivism: Theory, perspectives, and practice.* New York: Teachers College Press.

Gabler, I. C., & Schroeder, M. (2003). *Constructivist methods: Engaged minds.* Boston: Allyn & Bacon.

Gall, M. D., & Gall, J. P. (1976). The discussion method. In N. L. Gage (Ed.), *Psychology of teaching methods* (NSSE 75th Yearbook, Part 1).

Gall, M. (1984). Synthesis of research on teachers' questioning. *Educational Leadership, 42*(3), 40–47.

Gallagher, S. A., Stepien, W. J., & Rosenthal, H. (1992). The effects of problem-based learning on problem solving. *Gifted Child Quarterly, 36*(4), 195–200.

Gallimore, R., & Tharp, R. (1990). Teaching mind in society: Teaching, schooling, and literate discourse. In L. C. Moll (Ed.), *Vygotsky and education: Instructional implications and applications of sociohistroical psychology* (pp. 173–201). Cambridge: Cambridge University Press.

Gardner, H. (1993). *Multiple intelligences: The theory in practice/A reader.* New York: Basic Books.

Gautreau, C. F. (2004). *PowerPoint as an interactive multimedia lesson.* Retrieved August 24, 2008 from: http://www.techlearning.com/story/showArticle.php?articleID=22101388.

Georgeson, T. G., Gann, C .G., & Nourse, S. W. (2003). *Effective methods of supervising student teachers in special education environments.* ERIC Document ED 482.

Gettinger, M., & Seibert, J. K. (2002). Contributions of study skills to academic competence. *School Psychology Review, 31*(3), 360–365.

Ghaith, G. (2003). The relationship between forms of instruction, achievement and perceptions of classroom climate. *Educational Research, 45*(1), 83–93.

Gibson, E., & Darron, C. (1999). Teaching statistics to a student who is blind. *Teaching of Psychology, 26*(2), 130–131.

Glenberg, A. M., Gutierrez, T., Levin, J. R., Japuntich, S., & Kaschak, M. P. (2004). Activity and imagined activity can enhance young children's reading comprehension. *Journal of Educational Psychology, 96*(3), 424–436.

Gordon, P. R., Rogers, A. M., & Comfort, A. M., Gavula, N., & McGee, B. P. (2001). A taste of problem-based learning increases achievement of urban minority middle-school students. *Educational Horizons, 79*(4), 171–175.

Graffam, B. (2003). Constructivism and understanding: Implementing the teaching for understanding framework. *The Journal of Secondary Gifted Education, 15*(1), 13–22.

Griffin, C. C., Malone, L. D., & Kameenui, E. J. (1995). Effects of graphic organizer instruction on fifth-grade students. *Journal of Educational Research, 89*(2), 98–107.

Grossman, R. (2009). Structures for facilitating student reflection. *College Teaching, 57*(1), 15–22.

Guastello, E. F., Beasley, T. M., & Sinatra, C. (2000). Concept mapping effects on science content comprehension of low-achieving inner-city seventh graders. *Remedial and Special Education, 21*(6), 356–365.

Haas, M. (2005, March) Teaching methods for secondary algebra: A meta-analysis of findings. National Association of Secondary School Principals. *NASSP Bulletin* 89642, 24–26.

Hake, R. R. (n.d.). *Interactive-engagement vs traditional methods: A six-thousand student survey of mechanics test data for introductory physics courses.* Retrieved December 23, 2008, from: http://www.physics.indiana.edu/~sdi/ajpv3i.pdf.

Hall, C. W. (2001). A measure of executive processing skills in college students. *College Student Journal, 35*(3), 442–450.

Hansen, S. (2004). A constructivist approach to project assessment. *European Journal of Engineering Education, 29*(2), 211–220.

Hardy, M. D. (1997). Von Glaserfeld's radical constructivism: A critical review. *Science& Education, 6*(1–2), 135–150.

Harpaz, I., Balik, C., & Ehrenfeld, M. (2004). Concept mapping: An educational strategy for advancing nursing education. *Nursing Forum, 39*(2), 27–30.

Harvey, S., & Goudvis, A. (2007). *Strategies that work: Teaching comprehension for understanding and engagement.* Portland, ME: Stenhouse.

Hay, D. B., Wells, H., & Kinchin, I. M. (2008). Quantitative and qualitative measures of student learning at university level. *Higher Education: The International Journal of Higher Education and Educational Planning, 56*(2), 221–239.

Henson, K. T. (2004). *Constructivist teaching strategies for diverse middle-level classrooms.* Boston: Allyn & Bacon.

Herron, J. F., & Major, C. H. (2004). Community college leaders' attitudes toward problem-based learning as a method for teaching leadership. *Community College Journal of Research and Practice, 28*(2/3), 805–821.

Hobby Industry Association. (2002). *Executive Summary: The academic value of hands-on craft projects in elementary schools.* Elmwood Park, NJ: Author.

Huang, H. M. (2002). Toward constructivism for adult learners in online learning environments. *British Journal of Educational Technology, 33*(1), 27–37.

Hubber, P. (2005). Secondary students' perceptions of a constructivist-informed teaching and learning environment for geometric optics. *Teaching Science, 51*(1), 26–29.

Hutchison, D. (2007, January/February). Video games and the pedagogy of place. *Social Studies, 98*(1), 5–40.

Hyerle, D. (2004). *Student successes with thinking maps®: School-based research, results, and models for achievement using visual tools.* Thousand Oaks, CA: Corwin Press.

Illinois Learning Standards. http://www.isbe.net/ils/.

Institute for Learner Centered Education. http://www.learnercentereded. org/.

Ives, B. (2007). Graphic organizers applied to secondary algebra instruction for students with learning disabilities. *Learning Disabilities Research & Practice, 22*(2), 110–118.

James, J. (1996). *Thinking in the future tense: A workout for the mind.* New York: Touchstone.

James, W. (1991). *Pragmatism.* Amherst, NY: Prometheus Books.

Jensen, E. (2006). *Enriching the brain: How to maximize every learner's potential.* San Francisco: Jossey-Bass.

Jensen, E. (1998). *Teaching with the brain in mind.* Alexandria, VA: Association for Supervision and Curriculum Development.

Johnson, D., Maruyama, G., Johnson, R., Nelson, D., & Skon, L. (1981). Effects of cooperative, competitive, and individualistic goal structures on achievement: A meta-analysis. *Psychological Bulletin, 89*(1), 47–62.

Kagan, S. (1994). *Cooperative learning.* San Clemente, CA: Kagan Publishing.

Kahn, E. (2007). Building fires: Raising achievement through class discussion. *English Journal, 96*(4), 16–18. Retrieved from Internet June 22, pp. 1–3.

Kamii, C. K. (with Houseman, L. B.). (2000). *Young children reinvent arithmetic: Implications of Piaget's theory* (2nd ed.). New York: Teachers College Press.

Kamii, C. (with Livingston, S. J.). (1994). *Young children continue to reinvent arithmetic—3rd grade: Implications of Piaget's theory.* New York: Teacher's College Press.

Katayama, A. D., & Crooks, S. M. (2003). Online notes: Differential effects of studying complete or partial graphically organized notes. *The Journal of Experimental Education, 71*(4), 293–312.

Kaufman, D. M. (2003, January). Applying educational theory in practice. *British Medical Journal, 326,* 213–216.

Kegan, R. (1994). *In over our heads: The mental demands of modern life.* Cambridge, MA: Harvard University Press.

Kierwa, K. A. (1985). Providing the instructor's notes: An effective addition to student notetaking. *Educational Psychologist, 20*(1), 33–39.

Kiewra, K. A., DuBois, N. F., C., Christian, D., & McShane, D. (1988). Providing study notes: Comparison of three types of notes for review. *Journal of Educational Psychology, 80*(4), 595–597.

Kim, J. S. (2005). The effects of a constructivist teaching approach on student academic achievement, self-concept, and learning strategies. *Asia Pacific Education Review, 6*(1), 7–19.

King, K., & Gurian, M. (2006). Teaching to the minds of boys. *Educational Leadership, 64*(1) 56–61.

Kobayashi, K. (2006). Combined effects of note-taking/-reviewing on learning and the enhancement through interventions: A meta-analytic review. *Educational Psychology, 26*(3), 459–477.

Koh, C.-H., Khoo, H. E., Wong, M. L., & Koh, D. (2008). The effects of problem-based learning during medical school on physician competency: A systematic review. *Canadian Medical Association Journal, 178*(1), 34–41.

Kornfeld, J., & Leyden, G. (2005). Acting out: Literature, drama, and connecting with history. *The Reading Teacher, 59*(3), 230–238.

Kornhaber, M., & Krechevsky, M. (1993). Engaging intelligence. In H. Gardner (Ed.), *Multiple intelligences: The theory in practice/A reader* (pp. 231–248). Durham: Basic Books.

Kraemer, B. (1996, March). *Meeting the needs of nontraditional students: Retention and transfer studies.* Paper presented at the Annual Meeting of the North Central Association, Chicago, IL.

Leinhardt, G. (1992). What research on learning tells us about teaching. *Educational Leadership, 49*(7), 20–25.

Levine, M. (2002). *A mind at a time.* New York: Simon & Schuster.

Levy, H. M. (2008). Meeting the needs of all students through differentiated instruction: Helping every child reach and exceed standards. *The Clearing House, 81*(4), 161–164.

Lord, T. R. (1997). A comparison between traditional and constructivist teaching in college biology. *Innovative Higher Education, 21*(3), 197–215.

Lownebraun, S., & Nolen, S. B. (1998). Implementing change in a research university: Constructivist team teaching in a general education teacher education program. [Electronic version]. *Teacher Education and Special Education, 21*(1), 34–46.

Lunar Outpost Coaching Learning Experience Design. (2009). Illinois Mathematics and Science Academy. Retrieved from: http://pbln.imsa.edu/model/problems/lunar2008/led/intro/index.html.

Magoon, A. J. (1977). Constructivist approaches in educational research. *Review of Educational Leaedership, 47*(4), 651–693.

Mahoney, M. J. (2003). *What is constructivism and why is it growing?* Retrieved April 10, 2005 from: http://www.constructivism123.com/What is constructivism.htm. Handout at 8th International Congress of Constructivism & Psychotherapy, Bari, Italy.

Mahoney, M. J. (1993). Introduction to special section: Theoretical developments in the cognitive psychotherapies. *Journal of Consulting and Clinical Psychology, 61*(2), 187–193.

Manigieri, J. N., & Block, C. C. (1996). *Power thinking for success.* Cambridge, MA: Brookline.

Magoon, A. J. (1977). Constructivist approaches in educational research. *Review of Educational Leadership , 47*(4), 651–693.

Marley, S. C., Levin, J. R., & Glenberg, A. M. (2007). Improving Native American children's listening comprehension through concrete representations. *Contemporary Educational Psychology, 32*(3), 537–550.

Marzano, R. (2007). *The art and science of teaching: A comprehensive framework for effective instruction.* Alexandria, VA: Association for Supervision and Curriculum Development.

Marzano, R. J. (1993). How classroom teachers approach the teaching of thinking. *Theory Into Practice, 32*(3), 154–160.

Marzano, R. J., Pickering, D. J., & Pollock, J. E. (2001). *Classroom instruction that works: Research-based strategies for increasing student achievement.* Alexandria, VA: Association for Supervision and Curriculum Development.

Mautone, P. D., & Mayer, R. E. (2007). Cognitive aids for guiding graph comprehension. *Journal of Educational Psychology, 99*(3), 640–652.

Mayer, R. E. (1989). Systematic thinking fostered by illustrations in scientific text. *Journal of Educational Psychology, 81*(2), 240–246.

McCagg, E. C., & Dansereau, D. F. (1991). A convergent paradigm for examining knowledge mapping as a learning strategy. *Journal of Educational Research, 84*(6), 317–324.

McNeil, N. M., & Jarvin, L. (2007). When theories don't add up: Disentangling the manipulatives debate. *Theory into Practice, 46*(4), 309–316.

Meltzer, B. (2000, March/April). Cheating the kids. *Library Talk,* 31–32.

Merkley, D. M., & Jeffires, D. (2000/2001). Guidelines for implementing a graphic organizer. *The Reading Teacher, 54*(1), 350–357.

Mesch, D., Johnson, D. W., & Johnson, R. (1988). Impact of positive interdependence and academic group contingencies on achievement. *Journal of Social Psychology, 128*(3), 345–352.

Metros, S. E. (2008). The educator's role in preparing visually literate learners. *Theory into Practice, 47,* 102–109.

Metzger, S. A. (2007). Pedagogy and the historical feature film: Toward historical literacy. *Film & History, 37*(2), 67–75.

Monroe, J. (2003). Writing and the disciplines. *Peer Review, 6*(1), 8–11.

Morrison, E. H., McLaughlin, C., & Rucker, L. (2002). Medical students' note-taking in a medical biochemistry course: An initial exploration. *Medical Education, 36*, 384–386.

Moses, N., Klein, H. B., & Altman, E. (2001). An approach to assessing and facilitating causal language in adults with learning disabilities based on Piagetian theory. *Journal of Learning Disabilities, 23*(4), 220–228.

National Center for Education Statistics. (2008). *What does the NAEP writing assessment measure?* U.S. Department of Education. Institute of Education Sciences. Retrieved June 14, 2008 from: http://nces.ed.gov/nationsreportcard/writing/whatmeasure.asp.

National Leadership Council for Liberal Education & America's Promise. (2007). *College learning for the new global century.* Retrieved May 26, 2008 from: http://www.aacu.org/advocacy/leap/documents/GlobalCentury_final.pdf.

National Research Council. (2002). *How people learn: Brain, mind, experience, and school.* Washington, DC: National Academy.

Neimeyer, R. A. (1993). An appraisal of constructivist psychotherapies. *Journal of Consulting and Clinical Psychology, 61*(2), 221–234.

Neimeyer, R. A. (1995). An invitation to constructivist psychotherapies. In R. Neimeyer & M. Mahoney (Eds.), *Constructivism in psychotherapy* (pp. 1–15). Washington, DC: American Psychological Association.

Nesbit, J. C., & Adesope, O. O. (2006). Learning with concept and knowledge maps: A meta-analysis. *Review of Educational Research, 76*(3), 413–448.

Newell, G. E., & Winograd, P. (1989). The effects of writing on learning from expository text. *Written Communications, 6*(2), 196–217.

Newmann, F. M., Byrk, A. S., & Nagaoka, J. K. (2001). *Authentic intellectual work and standardized tests: Conflict or coexistence? Improving Chicago's schools.* Chicago: Consortium on Chicago School Research.

Nichols, J. D. (1996, October). The effects of cooperative learning on student achievement and motivation in a high school geometry class. *Contemporary Educational Psychology, 21*(4), 467–476.

Nichols, J. D., & Miller, R. B. (1994). Cooperative learning and student motivation. *Contemporary Educational Psychology, 19*, 167–178.

Nidds, J., & McGerald, J. (1995). Corporations view public education. *Education Digest, 61*(2), 27–28.

Nietfeld, J. L., Cao, L., & Osborne, J. W. (2005). Metacognitive monitoring accuracy and student performance in the postsecondary classroom. *The Journal of Experimental Education, 74*(1), 7–28.

Nuthall, G. (1999). The way students learn: Acquiring knowledge from an integrated science and social studies unit. *The Elementary School Journal, 99*(4), 303–340.

Oldfather, P. (1993). What students say about motivating experiences in a whole language classroom. *The Reading Teacher, 46*(8), 672–681.

Osman, M. E., & Hannafin, M. J. (1994). Effects of advance questioning and prior knowledge on science learning. *Journal of Educational Research, 88*(1), 5–13.

Overy, R. (1995). *Why the Allies won.* New York: W.W. Norton & Company.

Ozgungor, S., & Guthrie, J. T. (2004). Interaction among elaborative interrogation, knowledge, and interest in the process of constructing knowledge from text. *Journal of Educational Psychology, 96*(3), 437–443.

Palkovitz, R. J. & Lore, R. K. (1980). Note taking and note review: Why students fail questions based on lecture material. *Teaching of Psychology, 7*(3), 159–161.

Paris, S. G., & Paris, A. H. (2001). Classroom application of research on self-regulated learning. *Educational Psychologist, 36*(2), 89–101.

Park, C. C. (1997). Learning style preferences of Korean, Mexican, Armenian-American, and Anglo students in secondary schools. *NASSP BULLETIN, 81*(103), 103–111.

Parks, R. P. (1999, Summer). Macro principles, powerpoint, and the internet: Four years of the good, the bad, and the ugly. *Journal of Economic Education,* 200–209.

Pelech, J., & Singer, R. (2007). The bridging question strategy. *Journal for the Practical Application of Constructivist Theory in Education, 2*(1), 1–14.

Peter D. Hart Associates. (2006, December). *How should colleges prepare students to succeed in today's global economy?* Washington, DC: Association of American Colleges and Universities.

Peters, M. (2000). Does constructivist epistemology have a place in nurse education? *Journal of Nursing Education, 39*(4), 166–172.

Piaget, J. (2001). *Piaget: The psychology of intelligence.* (M. Piercy & D. E. Berlyne, Trans.). New York: Routledge. (Original work published 1947).

Popkewitz, T. S. (1998). Dewey, Vygotsky, and the social administration of the individual: Constructivist pedagogy as systems of ideas in historical spaces. *American Educational Research Journal, 55*(4), 535–570.

Porter, J. C. (1995, July). Constructivist learning. *Journal of Professional Issues in Engineerig Education and Practice,* 204–205.

Pribyl, J. R., & Bodner, G. M. (1987). Spatial ability and its role in organic chemistry: A study of four organic courses. *Journal of Research in Science Teaching, 24*(3), 229–240.

Pugalee, D. K. (2001). Algebra for all: The role of technology and constructivism in an algebra course for at-risk students. *Preventing School Failure, 45*(4), 171–176.

Raphael, D., & Wahlstrom, M. (1989). The influence of instruction aids on mathematics achievement. *Journal for Research in Mathematics Education, 20*(2), 173–190.

Rayneri, L. J., Gerber, B. L., & Wiley, L. P. (2006). The relationship between classroom environment and the learning style preference of gifted middle school students and the impact on levels of performance. *Gifted Child Quarterly, 50,* 104–118.

Redfield, D. L., & Rousseasu, E. W. (1981). A meta-analaysis of experimental research on teacher questioning behavior. *Review of Educational Research, 51*(2), 237– 245.

Reed, R. F., & Johnson, T. W. (2000). *Philosophical documents in education* (2nd ed.). New York: Longman.

Reich, R. (1992). *The work of nations.* New York: Vintage Books.

Reinhardt, L. (1999). Confessions of a "techno teacher." *College Teaching, 47*(2), 48–50.

Renaud, R., & Murray, H. (2007). The validity of higher-order questions as a process indicator of educational quality. *Research in Higher Education, 48*(3), 319– 351.

Rezvan, S., Ahmadi, S.A., & Abedi, M. R. (2006). The effects of metacognitive training on the academic achievement and happiness of Esfahan University conditional students. *Counseling Psychology Quarterly, 19*(4), 415–428.

Ritchie, D., & Gimenez, F. (1995/1996). Effectiveness of graphic organizers in computer- based instruction with dominant Spanish-speaking and dominant English-speaking students. *Journal of Research on Computing in Education, 28*(2), 221–234.

Robinson, D. H., Odom. A. B., Hsieh, Y., Vanderveen, A., & Katayma, A. D. (2006). Increasing text comprehension and graphic note taking using a partial graphic organizer. *The Journal of Educational Research, 100*(2), 103–111.

Roman, H. T. (2003). Multi-dimensional thinking: The key to the future. *Technology Teacher, 62*(5), 21–23.

Rorty, R. (1991). *Objectivism, relativism, and truth.* New York: Cambridge University.

Saphier, J., & Haley, M. A. (1993a). *Activators: Activity structures to engage students' thinking before Instruction.* Acton, MA: Research for Better Teaching.

Saphier, J., & Haley, M. A. (1993b). *Summarizers: Activity structures to support integration and retention of new learning.* Acton, MA: Research for Better Teaching.

Saxe, G. (1985). Effects of schooling on arithmetic understandings: Studies with Oksapmin children in Papua New Guinea. *Journal of Educational Psychology, 77*(5), 503–513.

Schattgen, S. F. (1997). From Piagetian theory to educational practice: Developing and Supporting constructivist early childhood teachers through Project Construct. *Journal of Early Childhood Teacher Education, 18*(2), 34–42.

Schwandt, T. A. (2003).Three epistemological stances for qualitative inquiry: Interpretivism, hermeneutics, and social constructionism. In N. K. Denzin & Y. S. Lincoln (Eds.), *The landscape of qualitative literature: Theories and issues* (pp. 292–331). Thousand Oaks, CA: Sage.

Seaman, T. (1990). *On the high road to achievement: Cooperative concept mapping.* ERIC document ED335140. Retrieved online September 8, 2008.

Shapiro, A. (2002). The latest dope on research (about constructivism); Part I: Different approaches to constructivism—what's it all about. International *Journal of Educational Reform, 11*(4), pp. 347–361.

Shaw, G., Brown, R., & Bromily, P. (1998). Strategic stories: How 3M is rewriting business planning. *Harvard Business Review, 76*(3), 41–50.

Simmons, D. C., Griffin, C. C., & Kameenui, E .J. (1988). Effects of teacher-constructed pre-and post-graphic organizer instruction in sixth-grade science students' comprehension and recall. *Journal of Educational Research, 82*(1), 15–21.

Snyder, R. F. (2000). The relationship between learning styles/multiple intelligences and academic achievement of high school students. *High School Journal, 83*(2), 11–20.

Sosa, D.A. (2006). *How the brain learns* (3rd ed.). Thousand Oaks, CA: Corwin.

Sowell, E. J. (1989). Effects of manipulative materials in mathematics instruction. *Journal for Research in Mathematics Education, 20*(5), 498–505.

Spigner-Littles, D., & Anderson, D. E. (1999). Constructivism: A paradigm for older learners. *Educational Gerontology, 25*, 203–209.

Stavridoou, F., & Kakana, D. (2008). Graphic abilities in relation to mathematical and scientific ability in adolescents. *Educational Research, 50*(1), 75–93.

Sternberg, R. J. (2007/2008). Assessing what matters. *Educational Leadership, 65*(4), 20–26.

Stevenson, L., & Haberman, D. L. (1998). *Ten theories of human nature.* Oxford: Oxford University Press.

Stodolsky, S. S., Ferguson, T. L., & Wimpelberf, K. (1981). The recitation persists, but what does it look like? *Journal of Curriculum Studies, 13*, 121–130.

Sungur, S., & Tekkaya, C. (2006). Effects of problem-based learning and traditional instruction on self-regulated learning. *The Journal of Educational Research, 99*(5), 307–317.

Taylor, A. E. (1955). *Aristotle.* New York: Dover Publications, Inc.

The Problem-based Learning Network at the Illinois Mathematics and Science Academy: http://pbln.imsa.edu.

3M Corporation, (2001). Polishing Your Presentation. Available at http://www.3m.com/meetingnetwork/readingroom/meetingguide_pres.html.

Tobias, C. U. (1994). *The way they learn.* Wheaton, IL.: Tyndale House.

Tomlison, C. A. (1999). *The differentiated classroom: Responding to the needs of all learners.* Alexandria, VA: Association for Supervision and Curriculum Development.

Tomlison, C. A. (1998, November). Teach me, teach my brain: A call for differentiated classrooms. *Educational Leadership*, 52–55.

Toomey, B., & Ecker, B. (2007). Of neurons and knowings: Constructivism, coherence psychology, and their neurodyanamic substrates. *Journal of Constructivist Psychology, 20*(3), 201–245.

Torp, L., & Sage, S. (2002). *Problems as possibilities: Problem-based learning for K-16 education* (2nd ed). Alexandria, VA: Association for Supervision and Curriculum Development.

Trainin, G., & Swanson, H.L. (2005). Cognition, metacognition, and achievement of college students with learning disabilities. *Learning Disability Quarterly, 28*, 261–272.

Trotter, A. (1995). Classroom constructivism. *The Executive Educator, 17*(10), 25–27.

Tufte, E. R. (2003). *The cognitive style of PowerPoint.* Chesire, CT: Graphics Press LLC.

USA Today—Sample Lesson Plans. http://www.usatoday.com/educate/lessons.htm.

Verriour, P. (1985). Face to face: Negotiating meaning through drama. *Electronic Theory Into Practice, 24*(3), 181–186.

Vermette, P. J. (1998). *Making cooperative learning work: Student teams in K-12 classrooms.* Upper Saddle River, NJ: Merrill Development.

Vernon, D. T., & Blake, R. L. (1993). Does problem-based learning work? A meta-analysis of evaluative research. *Academic Medicine, 68*(7), 550–563.

Viadero, D. (2007). Studies find that use of learning toys can backfire. *Education Week, 26*(34), 12–13.

Von Glaserfeld, E. (2005). Introduction: Aspects of constructivism. In C. T. Fosnot (Ed.), *Constructivism: Theory, perspectives, and practice* (pp. 3–7). New York: Teachers College Press.

Vygotsky, L. S. (Ed.). (1962). *Thought and language.* Cambridge, MA: MIT Press.

Walsh, J. A., & Sattes, B. D. (2005). *Quality questioning: Research-based practice to engage every learner.* Thousand Oaks, CA: Corwin & AEL: A Joint Publication.

Wannagat, U. (2007). Learning though L2-content and language integrated learning (CLIL) and English as medium of instruction (EMI). T*he International Journal of Bilingual Education and Bilingualism, 10*(5), 663–680.

Webster, P. (2000). Reforming secondary music teaching in the new century. *Journal of Secondary Gifted Education, 12*(1), 17–24.

Wiggins, G., & McTighe, J. (2006). Examining the teaching life. *Educational Leadership, 63*(6), 26–29.

Willis, J. (2006). *Research-based strategies to ignite student learning.* Alexandria, VA: Association for Supervision and Curriculum Development.

Wilson-Jones, L., & Caston, N. C. (2004). Cooperative learning on academic achievement in elementary African American males. *Journal of Instructional Psychology, 31*(4), 280–283.

Woloshyn, V. E., Wood, E., Willouoghby, T., & Pressley, M. (1990). Elaborative interrogation facilitates adult learning of factual paragraphs. *Journal of Educational Psychology, 82*(3), 513–524.

Wood, E., Prressley, M., & Winne, P. H. (1990). Elaborative interrogation effects on children's learning of factual content. *Journal of Educational Psychology, 82*(4), 741–748.

Wolfe, P. (2001). *Brain matters: Translating research into classroom practice.* Alexandria, VA: Association for Supervision and Curriculum Development.

Zehr, D. (2004). Two active learning exercises for a history of psychology class. *Teaching of Psychology, 31*(1), 54–56.

Zhining, Q., Johnson, D. W., & Johnson, R. T. (1995). Cooperative versus competitive efforts and problem solving. *Review of Educational Research, 65*(2), 129–143. Retrieved form the Internet 3/12/2007.

Zimmerman, B.J. (2002). Becoming a self-regulated learner: An overview. *Theory into Practice, 41*(2), 64–70.

LaVergne, TN USA
15 October 2010
201040LV00001B/9/P